The Publishing Lab
Student Creative Work
Volume 1, Spring 2024

Photo: Elyse Rosenberg

The Publishing Lab
Student Creative Work
Volume 1, Spring 2024

Published by Pace University Press
41 Park Row
New York, NY 10038

ISSN: 2996-5993
ISBN: 978-1-935625-83-4

Cover Design by Kayleigh Woltal
Cover Photo by Kayleigh Woltal

Printed in the United States of America

Acknowledgments

The Publishing Lab Team would like to thank all our contributors for embarking with us on this new project. We were thrilled to work with all of you.

We also thank our advisors, Professor Manuela Soares and Professor Eileen Kreit. We couldn't have succeeded with *The Publishing Lab* if it weren't for their trust and support.

A special thank you to Kayleigh Woltal for taking on this project and making terrific work with this issue's design.

Thank you to everybody at Pace University Press for your help with the logistics of putting a physical book together.

To each member of *The Publishing Lab*, both in our editorial and marketing teams, you were amazing!

And to our next generation of students who are embracing *The Publishing Lab*. This is a project created to give the MS in Publishing students at Pace University an opportunity gain hands-on experiential learning about publishing in a safe and encouraging environment. Thank you for committing to bring this project to a next generation of publishing students!

TABLE OF CONTENTS

Welcome to the Publishing Lab!

Publishing is a highly creative industry that attracts imaginative people to every department. Though the creative content is brought in by the editors, everyone works to market and sell that content in innovative and inspired ways.

Our publishing students are passionate about books and are avid readers and often, writers. This outlet for their creativity in the program was inspired by the students themselves and organized and led by a small cohort who have acquired, edited, copyedited, proofread, and designed this volume.

Students who are both in person and online contributed to the success of this anthology in many ways. There are twenty-one student authors who submitted their writing and photography, and ten Publishing Lab board members who worked on every aspect of the bookmaking process: getting their fellow students to send in their work, editing, marketing, and social media.

Working with our students on this endeavor has been a truly enlightening and enjoyable experience. We are proud of their work in the program and equally proud of their creative endeavors as demonstrated by this book.

Enjoy the first volume of *The Publishing Lab*.

Manuela Soares

Director, MS in Publishing Program
Director, Pace University Press

Eileen Bishop Kreit

Lecturer and Faculty Advisor, MS in Publishing Program
Faculty Advisor, Pace University Press

Preface | The Publishing Lab

The Publishing Lab was created by students of the Pace University MS in Publishing program. When I brought the idea forward to Professor Soares, I was thrilled to be received with such excitement. She said, "Find us four more students that are on board, someone in faculty to be your advisor, and let's get started."

The Publishing Lab allowed us to experiment, to learn hands-on, and to become better editors. It also brought us the opportunity to get to know some of our colleagues who study remotely from many corners of the United States, and to discover the fantastic writers we have in the program.

All the works you will read in this anthology were written and edited by Pace MS in Publishing students. From poetry to prose, our authors take us through sweet and bittersweet romance, through YA fiction, through magical realism, through worlds like ours and fantastical universes.

Working with *The Publishing Lab* has been a wonderful adventure. I am beyond thankful for the support of the Publishing program for new ideas like this one. I would also like to leave a special thank you for Professor Soares, Professor Kreit, and my colleagues Amber Grell, Harshdeep Kaur, Kaitlyn Keel, and Shianne Henion. Thank you all for working to bring this idea to life. It is because of your trust that now our program has even more possibilities for its students to develop the skills they need to achieve their dream careers.

I'd like to thank our team as well: Kristen Mejia, Sam Semerau, Pand Milo, Elyse Rosenberg, Mary Jane Duffy, and Kayleigh Woltal. This book wouldn't be here without your work.

This anthology is the first issue of a project that we hope will be a legacy to future generations of Pace MS in Publishing students. Enjoy your reading!

Luiza Guimarães
Editor-in-Chief, *The Publishing Lab*

The Publishing Lab
Student Creative Work
Volume 1, Spring 2024

MS in Publishing Program, Pace University

Magazines
by Camille Daniels

Stories,

Topics,

Pictures,

Ads,

Teamwork,

Deadlines,

Legacies,

Impact,

Controversies,

Boundaries pushed,

Features,

Profiles,

Investigations,

Representation,

Human examination,

One-word names,

Article styles,

An entire industry,

Always for the people,

Some who know how to read, others who don't,

Made art inspiring, a connector to all,

Invited conversations to be had,

Creators to come together,

One goal, one theme, one mission,

Read, inspire, teach, educate,

Pages coated with gloss,

Some filled with only news

Once fat per issue,

Now thin or simply nonexistent,

Digital has caused print to step back,

And now we rely on memory,

The days when the issue was mailed to you,

Or you bought it in person at the newsstand,

Now they're replaced by tabloids,

Gone are the wall-to-wall issues—only to find them barely in the grocery checkout

Or maybe in a specialty store,

No longer are they everywhere,

And what a shame that is,

That there hasn't been a way to celebrate both the print and digital

To recognize that both are needed, both are essential,

Both offer something that one alone can't,

Oh, how they continue to amaze, magazines.

Peace Be Still

by Camille Daniels

Clutter,
Declutter,
Organize,
Disorganize,
Paper, plastic, stuff,
Memories in closets,
Shelves filled with books and bills,
Things just pile up,
Madness and sadness,
Newspapers on the stand,
Magazines on the couch,
Books on the floor, some open, some closed,
How does it get this way?
Where is the peace?
The order?
The purpose?
How did we get here?
And how do we turn this thing around?
Design, says create,
It represents hope,
It represents invention,
A reminder that there is another way to live,
A life that involves order,
Peace and purpose,
Clarity for the mind,
A calmness for the soul,
This is what happens when the clothes are folded,

And things are put away,
Not too many books,
Not too many magazines,
Not too many newspapers,
Not too many "important papers,"
Just order,
Just peace,
Just decluttering,
To kill the chaos,
To kill the spirit that is the action of clutter,
Sun shines in,
The fresh air greets,
Peace be still and it resides,
On these cool, colored, and fresh sheets.

Swift Rejection

by Camille Daniels

It happened so suddenly,

Words were exchanged at a time that none should have been spoken,

Yet they were,

A mind clouded with thoughts,

An energy filled with frustration and rage,

Were taken out on someone who simply hit "send."

The response was swift,

The previous energy dissipated,

And one of remorse quickly took its place,

Now there is a block,

A pause of sorts,

Maybe for a lifetime or maybe for a moment,

Oh, the power of a moment,

The power of an email,

Poor judgment can leave an impact even in a matter of moments,

A lesson is learned,

And a scar is formed in the form of an email,

Good and bad occur in the matter of a moment,

All to remind us,

Take a moment before speaking,

Let the energy from one moment completely leave before moving on to the next,

No one is ever completely at their best from moment to moment,

And to have more of good than bad,

Remember to take a breath,

Remember we're all human,

Forgive ourselves for what we've done,

Learn from it and move on,

And pray that the next time can be as good a moment
as anyone could have.

Cross Point

by Camille Daniels

How do you let go?

How do you know when to surrender?

How do you make peace?

When do you say goodbye to an identity?

Are you a failure for trying?

Have you just been lying?

How do you justify only going so far?

How do you define success, when you end up adjacent to it?

Time spent, feelings hurt,

Worth questioned,

Sanity tested

These are the questions that no one can explain the answers for

All your questions go answered,

But only you can answer them,

And that can be hard as the result is the same

You must live with consequences,

Accept the time that has been spent,

And hope to God something good comes from days, weeks, and hours that were given to this thing that was the object of your pursuit.

Insecurity

by Camille Daniels

Your presence invokes something in me,

An anger, a jealousy,

You cannot be beaten,

You cannot be broken,

How can that be?

Are you not human?

Have you somehow figured out how to outdo
mortality?

How is this possible?

I wish something would break you,

Make you crumble,

The joy of your defeat would bring a smile to my face,

Why must I see you suffer?

Because it would prove one thing to be true,

You're no different,

You too are indeed human,

You can indeed be broken,

Your bravado, is just that, a show,

We all hurt, even you,

You may be able to beat me,

But you are no different than I,

You have your demons,

Just like the rest of us,

You too will be judged when your time comes,

Just like the rest of us,

But why you invoke this emotion,

How you tap into my feelings of less than,

I do not know,

But then I am reminded,

That what makes you, you,

Is the thing that we all have that you have so wonderfully masked,

You became the thing,

That so many of us want to be,

By using the thing that made you worse,

And turned into your best,

So, I will too, follow you, in doing the same,

Take my worst and make it my best,

And whether I see you in the box or not,

I know that we are the same,

You chose your weapon,

And I have done the same,

I may have my feelings, and yes you bring them out of me,

But the truth is we are indeed the same.

The Café Dating Dance
by Kayleigh Woltal

The café dating dance continues.

He waits at the other end of the bench as she endures another disaster, abandoning his homework as always when failed date number twelve finally leaves. He watches as she buries her head in her hands and drowns her sorrows in the sweetest drink on the menu when the exit bell chimes. He asks her for the highlights, and she snaps at him, but after three long sips she gives in.

"This one somehow confused Linkin Park and One Direction."

He gathers his notebooks and scoots over to her table, laughing at her misfortune as if watching her go on these stupid dates isn't killing him inside—as if he doesn't want to scream, "I'm right here. I always have been."

He ignores the familiar ache in his chest and teases.

"Admit it. I will forever be your best date. A first grader managed to ruin other guys forever. That's some real skill."

"You yanked me under a slide and gave me a weed," she reminds him.

"It wasn't a *weed*; it was a dandelion! Those are flowers."

"Those are *weeds*."

"Well, at least I chose the blue slide. I could have brought you to the yellow one with the spiders."

He wants to tell her that it wasn't about the spiders. In kindergarten, she got pushed down the yellow slide and had burns on her elbows for days, and he remembered how she cried. He didn't want his special moment with her to be connected to the slide that made her cry. He never tells her any of this.

"Such a gentleman," she mocks now with a grin.

He looks forward to seeing her face light up as if it's the first time he's ever seen it. They go through the same bout of banter time after time, but he still swears it feels like something new.

§

She rolls her eyes like it's her version of breathing and calls him by his full name to piss him off, putting his teasing to rest for the day.

Week after week, she feels him stealing glances at her while her date tells her about himself, and she tries her best to ignore him when he wiggles his eyebrows at her over his laptop. She lies to herself and says she wishes he would leave her alone. But then she remembers the day he couldn't be there and the disappointing pang she felt deep in her chest.

The truth is, she loves his teasing her about their childhood flirtation, and she loves to fight back with the flower/weed debate, and she loves when he wiggles his eyebrows at her because it all means he's there with her.

She'll never give him the satisfaction, but she knows that childhood date truly was the best date she had ever been on.

Deep down they both know the *real* dating dance is between the two of them.

Yellow Dress

by Nina Hook

I delicately picked up the scattered stones
Smooth from the impact of your throw
Again and again the erosion began
What once was jagged and sharp
Became smooth and soft and round

I gently bent down and cradled them in my hands
A little trail I followed, carefully placed by you
Only to feel trapped as I reached the end
Where the cliff ran down
And the water screamed
My name
Caught in the back of your throat
A bloody sore that hurts so good
That is what I am to you
A wound that you cannot sew shut
A hurt that runs freely in your veins
A vice aimed to kill, a slow suffering by your own will

My pale yellow slip dress soaked up the sun
As the shadows of my toned, tan thighs danced in the
autumn leaves
You could see the crevice of my side
And my eyes pleaded
Soft stones in my hands
You on my hips
My skin burned like a wildfire and spread throughout, a
fiery red

Caught on your cheeks in small, shy patches

I had never seen a boy so smitten

Yet you dealt me roughly like a misbehaving card deck

My luck had never been good, and your strategy far too predictable

The shadows danced in between my dress

The sun eavesdropped through the branches

Your hands played under my silk, a choreographed dance

That you had done so well before

A standing ovation I would've given

If my legs stood a chance

I yearned for this lust in my dreams the night before

But awoke before I came, and neither did the love

Now you were solid, a pearly silhouette on my berry stained lips

Yet I knew that you would run and hide

Once the moon arrived

The tide would pull you back

And I would be alone with the stars and the sky

And the night would swallow me with no apology or remorse

Alone and lonely; solitude greeted me like an older sister

"Flâneuse" they whispered to me in a minor key

That my ears found so hauntingly sweet

I knew I would wander back to you, retracing my light steps

With my pretty shadow twirling right behind

You would take me in your arms, freckles stamping on my skin

As you traced your love back down my stomach

And whisked it away with your lips pressed into my chocolate hair

I forcefully skipped the stones in the river by the cottage

The yellow boards of the house matched my dress

The lace reflected the design on the window boards

The smooth stones elegantly danced on the water

As I knew you would be back, then swallowed again

The sun and the moon, my dear old friends

A Promise to Her

by Michaela MacFarran

This place smells like Halloween and feels like home

One day I'll bring her here

We'll walk hand and hand up the crooked, cracked sidewalk and look into the homes too rich for our blood

Imagining a life without worry, without stress, without the pain of living in a world with so much uncertainty

We'll wake up on weekends to the sun finding its way into our bedroom, a welcome visitor in our tiny oasis

Coffee will be poured and pancakes will be made, while love songs of yesteryear fill the air with a vibrance once seemingly unattainable—though no singular note sung by even the Earth's most talented songstress could ever match the beauty of the sound of life with her

And then she'll leave for a time, to share her gift with people too stubborn to know that she is a gift in itself —to even hear her is the definition of grace—to even begin to understand her is passion at its most basic form

And I'll sit and walk and write, desperate to make something out of a life once clouded by nothingness . . . But that desperation will dissolve as the days turn to weeks turn to months, and the love of the thing once lost to the mundaneness of the nine to five will fuel the will of life—the meaning behind it all

And she'll return

And she'll tell me about her day and I'll do the same, and regardless of happy or sad, angry or calm, the underlying knowledge that despite hardship, the peace of home will always be found within each other will be the why

One day I'll bring her here

September 21

by Michaela MacFarran

I like to watch people in love. Every night on my commute home from work, I see the same couple. Not in face or name. But in the way they hold each other, arm over shoulder, hand in hand. Their heads pressed together in a tired comfort. They never speak. It's far too late for words.

At first, I thought these couples were in a sad state of goodbye. Clinging to the last few minutes before they have to get off at their respective train stops, saying farewell to the time they spent building their relationship. Now I see it as a different type of melancholy. The type you can only feel in the quiet moments this city allows you to have. I've felt it on the Staten Island Ferry. No matter the time. No matter the company. There's something about looking at a city prided on its sleeplessness that makes it all the more still once you're pulling away from it.

I look to my right and smile. As if I'm smiling at the person I share this same silent love with. She's not there though. No matter how many times I turn and think she is, I'm met with a state of blankness. Both in the physicality of the space I inhabit and in the eyes of those I thought looked at me the same way. I can't help but sigh and think this type of melancholy, while beautiful, is better shared between lovers than cursed upon the lonely.

Cherry Blossom

by Shannon Huurman

There's a cherry tree I pass
everyday on my way to work.
It reminds me of us—
the way we would lay outside under trees
reading, writing, laughing,
understanding one another.
Until we didn't.
The cherry,
most like us
the way it blooms.
Bright, pink flowers one day
then quickly, the flowers are gone and
only green leaves remain.
No trace that the flowers were ever there.

Touch

by Hannah Penn

There is a dangerous belief
of love sweetened
by touch.
Forever beginning
with a sense of familiarity,
real or not real.
A lovely deception
in this simple game
of blindly following sensation.
The tangling of limbs
and whispered promises
of eternity.
A light in the dark,
relishing in the comfort
of touch.

Unraveling

by Hannah Penn

Isn't it crazy
how after years apart,
you can look at someone,
and what once was dead
is suddenly reborn?
Is that not
the craziest thing?

We are told that the past
is definite.
Defining moments that
cannot be reversed.
And they're not undone,
but instead we can now learn.

Forgive and forget.
Or do neither.
Acknowledge what has been done
and undo the pain you hold.
Easier said than done,
that much is true.

You are as familiar to me
as the loose thread
on my sweater.
I tug on that thread
until it unravels,
and I'll do the same
with you and I.

A Day in the Life of a Commuter
by Shay Blackthorn

I think about dying. A lot. Okay, not like literally dying, but killing the part of my brain that doesn't shut up. There are moments when that voice, who I call Jeremy, commands me to commit heinous acts because he thinks I should.

I drive across the Newburgh-Beacon Bridge every day to catch the train to New York, and every time I am halfway across, Jeremy tells me to drive into the Hudson River. It's to the point now where I expect him.

It always goes something like this:

There I am, headed towards the opposite end of the bridge. Jeremy, who doesn't have an actual face but a voice as smooth as if he were an audiobook narrator, bloops into my head. "Good morning, Joe, please end your life. You are meaningless to all people."

To which I reply, "Why, hello Jeremy. Did someone start their day without coffee again?"

"Do you remember that time when your aunt, upon telling her you didn't feel good, asked if you were going to kill yourself?"

"I was hungover, Jeremy."

"And that didn't stop her from asking, did it? It's that obvious everyone is waiting for that phone call, champ."

It is at this point in the drive I grip my steering wheel and angrily roll my eyes as some dickhead in a 2009 Dodge Ram—that is so rusted it should've been junked years ago—zooms past my Subaru because he hates that I'm in front of him. I give him the finger.

"I haven't had suicidal thoughts since I was 19. I am almost 23. I think they can set the phone down," I shoot back at Jeremy. "Leave me alone." Then I turn up the stereo, which is usually some song by Taylor Swift.

"Remember when Shaun left you for his stalker? You are that unbearable."

And that is when I wish I could kill the thing called Jeremy. It is not enough for him to remind me of old and slightly painful memories, but the most recent one? Come *on*. I still sob to "All Too Well (10-Minute Version) (Taylor's Version)" and Jeremy knows that. Jeremy knows a lot of things about me. He is like the worst best friend you could ever have, the one who calls themselves brutally honest when really, they're just an asshole.

I don't want to think about Shaun on some random Tuesday while crossing the Hamilton Fish into Beacon. I don't want to remember when my mental health was so severe, my family rarely spoke to me.

I, a 23-year-old teenage girl, want to get on the 11:02 train, stare out the window solemnly, and pretend I am about to enter my rom-com era.

I love pretending. I love the idea of someone watching me as I read in my seat, my coffee in hand. I love to imagine my hair falling into my face and I do that super casual move where I tuck it behind my ear. And then I look up and catch them staring at me, and their eyes are glued to my own, and then fireworks explode because *finally* this bitch has someone who thinks she is *hot*.

But shit doesn't work that way, and Jeremy reminds me of that, too. As I park and pay, Jeremy oh-so tells me that my stomach looks horrendous in this top and that if anyone looks at me it is to gawk and think "*Oh, she is sooo big!*" to themselves as I sit down, or "*Why is she eating a muffin when she should be eating a salad?*" And as I start my trek to the platform, I am reminded that I haven't completed my exercise rings since March of 2022.

I don't buy a muffin today. I can wait till lunch for something to eat, and then if I get dinner, I'll only have had two meals today. Which is *great*. I do buy a coffee though, and I make sure it's light and almost sweet. I still like that coffee taste, just not as bitter. I worry about when my coffee is an overkill of sugar, and what my grandmother would say if she saw how much I poured into my cup. The guy at the counter, who knows me by name, smiles and asks how I'm doing.

Whenever someone asks me how I'm doing, I have that moment where I feel like Bella Swan in *New Moon*, with Ghost Edward behind her hissing "*Lie! Lie better!*" So, I tell the cashier I've been doing really good.

He offers me a genuine smile, and I feel a sense of accomplishment. If people think I'm doing great, then it must be true.

The train is usually empty at my station, so I have no problem finding a window seat. Beyond needing the window, I am particular about my spot. I can't sit directly across or behind someone, always needing at least a seat apart from strangers. This is easy for me to accomplish, too. I set my bag down, then my coffee, and finally myself. I get comfortable. I pull out my book, and make sure my ticket is ready for my conductor. And then I let myself pretend.

There is a house in between the Tarrytown and Irvington stations that I am obsessed with. It has a step-style roof with orange shingles, and these old white walls. Foliage grows up its side during the spring and summer seasons. My favorite part is this small shed tucked away, down the hill and against the woods. Imagine a house full of secrets and beauty, its smooth cream stone holding so much within its walls, then this dilapidated, beaten-to-shit shack, hidden from view. I pause my reading every time to look out my window at it, and mentally, I tell both buildings hello.

"Wouldn't it be funny if this train crashed? You know there was an accident in 2012 where the train was moving too fast and when it came to the bend near Spuyten Duyvil, it fell on its side," Jeremy whispered, because he knows better than to talk loudly while I read.

I close my eyes for a moment, pinch the bridge of my nose, and go back to reading, trying my best not to overanalyze the sudden rockiness of the train.

"What if the guy behind you grabs you by your hair? What will you do? What if you get back to Beacon and your car is stolen, or worse, on fire? What if you get into the city and realize you don't have your student ID? What if someone rips your bag out of your hands? What if you get a call saying someone broke into your house and kidnapped the dogs? What if Matthew doesn't come inside tonight and gets eaten by a coyote?"

Matthew, my super old orange cat, knows better than to be eaten by a coyote. He was born and raised in a garbage truck yard.

I tell Jeremy this, but then he laughs. "Oh, but you know it could happen.

Or someone with a personal vendetta against you since high school could decide today is the day for revenge."

I try to turn my music up, but it's as if Jeremy puts his hand on mine and stops me.

"No, Joe. You need to listen to me. Listen to what I'm saying to you. These are not impossible things. You need to prepare for the worst. Your grandpa could die."

"My grandpa is fine," I say, but my voice is wobbly. After all, Jeremy is right. These things technically *could* happen . . . but there is a high probability that they won't. Right? I once overheard a conversation between my grandparents, where he said he probably only has twenty years of his life left. My grandpa is 64. But twenty years . . . that's only a short amount of time. So much he won't be there to see. I'll forget the sound of his laugh, I'll have to watch him be buried, I will have to exist in this world where he's in the ground—

"Grand Central, our final destination. Track 23 upper-level. Have a great day!"

I slam my book shut, shove it into my bag, and race off the train. This time, Jeremy can't stop me from turning up my music and luckily, it's something loud and heavy. By the time I make it to the subway, I'm winded, but I catch the 5 Train downtown. I'm squished like a sardine, my bookbag is stuffed with my schoolbooks and lunch, and as my music blares, I can feel Jeremy etch along my skull, "Everyone HATES you because you take up so much space."

But I do not have time for Jeremy. I have to go to work.

"Oh, so you don't want to know what they think?"

"No, not really."

My fingers tap against my leg, and I check my stance, opting to move in closer to the center pole in the car.

"But Joe, it matters. Don't you want to fit in? To stop being known as that weird fat girl? This is your chance! If you look around, and I mean it," Jeremy snaps his fingers. *"Look around. Look at how they don't even look at you. It's because if they do, they'll vomit. All over you. Maybe even on*

your shoes." My stop approaches. "Now get off the train so they can have some space."

I take the elevator to the street because I did my makeup today and I want to preserve it as much as possible. But guilt gnaws at me as I do. The elevator is for people who can't use the stairs, not for fat and lazy girls like me. Jeremy seconds that point.

It isn't often that I feel that urge to yell, but the incessant chatter bugs me to no end. I want to break something, probably my phone. But I am weak with little muscles and can barely snap a pencil.

"Jeremy," I begin. "What will it take for you to stop talking?"

Jeremy pauses for a moment, then takes a deep breath. "The fact you would even say that to me is so upsetting, Joe. I thought we were friends?"

I gnaw on my bottom lip. "You said you hated me yesterday and wished ill on my cat. How could we be friends after that?"

"Because you need someone who tells you how it is, Joe. Imagine if everyone you met was nice to you. That would be disgusting. You need pain in your life, and there is no one more suited to the task than me! You love my brutal honesty because it's your armor against the world. I keep you safe, my love."

"You keep me safe . . ." I echo. "Then why don't I ever feel safe with you?"

Jeremy pauses for a moment. "Because you don't trust me, deep down. But our bond is something that will take time, so long as you understand that I am the only honest person you will meet in your life. I promise."

I consider Jeremy for a second, with his deep baritone and his soft lilt of words. I can picture him so clearly in my head now, the only hand that's ever remained outstretched for me to take. Everyone else in my life has left, whether it be my own fault or theirs, or a combination of both. I recall Holly and our friendship that was doomed before it began, or Lindsay, who kept a chart of all the times I owed her money. I recall the moment I went to leave my house, and my grandmother stopped me in my tracks and asked when I was going to do something about my stomach.

Jeremy's hand was reaching for mine, but I pulled away and formed it into a fist. Jeremy never told me I was beautiful, or that my body was gorgeous as it was. He never encouraged me to chase my dreams, or that I should celebrate my good grades and when I did something good at work. He indulged in those worse parts of myself, and he thought I should reward him for that. Just like how so many people desired awards for the times they caused me pain.

"What's wrong?" Jeremy asks now, his hand pushing my hair back from my face. My office building is coming up now, and I cross the street passing a vendor selling gyros. "Why won't you speak to me, Joe?"

I decide to ignore him. I walk into my office building and shove Jeremy so far down I can feel him banging on my rib cage like it's his own personal jail. For a moment, everything is hazy, like a dance party with too much fog machine. But then I step up the elevator and wait for it to take me up to the sky.

A Winter Day at the Shore
by Shannon Huurman

I sat along the shore for so long,
writing verses,
meditating.
I watched the waves reach closer
and create tide pools just past my feet.
Suddenly,
it was night.

The Magnolia Tree in My Front Yard Reminds Me I'm Not Finished Yet
by Shannon Huurman

Texas—so green in the summer
life continues through
oppressive heat.
Maybe I was always
meant to flourish in August—
like the magnolia—
to bloom when others wilt.

You Told My Mom You Would Walk Me Home
by Shannon Huurman

You told my mom
you would walk me home.
But four hours later,
when I said, "I'm going to head home,"
you didn't even budge.
You must have forgotten you had even said anything.
So now you don't think I am even
worth walking home. I know I was once.
While I walked
I thought,
If anything were to happen,
Cause let's face it,
I'm a small girl
walking alone in New York after dark,
I could be grabbed by my ponytail,
dragged into a dark corner,
walking with keys between my knuckles
couldn't save me.
I'm mutilated and raped.
Left for dead.
It's possible;
Definitely more likely than you may think.
Of course you'd feel bad!
Some ounce of guilt!
What would you do if my mom said,
"You told me you would walk her home."

Medusa's Monday

by Kayleigh Woltal

The man with the camera sits on the last spot of the subway bench closest to the doors. I don't pay him much attention. I am already running late for work after a weekend from hell.

It was the weekend of my cousin's wedding, an event I was already dreading which seemed to cause every inconvenience imaginable. From the moment I stepped foot into Penn Station to head home, everything went downhill. I stopped at the Starbucks while waiting for my track announcement, and the barista managed to elbow a cup on the counter I was leaning against, covering me in nearly boiling coffee. I stood in the station, reeking of coffee beans, and watched as my train got pushed back again and again due to snow delays. It took me nearly three hours to get home.

If the bad luck had ended in Penn, I would have been alright. I wouldn't have felt the familiar desire to unleash the monster within me. But that wasn't the case. My zipper ripped in the middle of the reception at the wedding, and I spent the rest of the night safety pinned up, being sure not to move in any way I could expose myself. In case the dress being ruined wasn't enough, my sister made sure to vomit all over the matching shoes as well. Open bar.

Today, I am done. I am exhausted, I am angry, I have far too long of a commute from my Inwood apartment to the office, and I am in no mood for any more tests of my patience.

The man on the bench steals my attention as he wraps his hands around the lens of the camera sitting idly on his lap. He squeezes at the cap, releasing it to reveal the shiny glass.

I look at him in warning: Don't look at me. Don't take pictures of me. *Don't make me angry.*

The man glances down at the camera's screen with just his eyes, as if not looking directly at it might make his actions less noticeable, as if I can't hear the shutter. I stare directly into the lens, but his facial expression remains the same. I hear the shutter click again, and I swear I see a slight curve of his lips.

You'd think that when you look them dead in the eye, they'd stop. You've caught them. It should be over. They should really have the sense that they're not being as sly as they think they are. But no, they always keep going, as if having you look at them makes the photo even better.

Somehow, knowing that there are now photos of me on that camera isn't what makes me want to lose it. It's that I know that if I were to rip the SD card right out of its slot, I would also find photos of dozens of other women innocently on their way to work, home, the grocery store, the theater . . .

I contemplate aiming my phone at him, taking my own little creepy keepsake, just to see how he likes it, but I'm far too angry to do something so petty now. I want to take real action.

The train doors open again, and a new batch of commuters step on board. 50th. One more stop. Just one more.

But it's too late. I feel the fury bubbling up inside of me.

I make direct eye contact with him this time. One last warning before I boil over.

He stares back at me and presses his finger down on the shutter button again. I let loose. I let go of the monster within, and she goes for the kill that's in her nature. The man slumps over in an instant, his fingers slacking on that stupid camera.

I watch as it topples out of his hand, drops down on the subway floor, skids through the aisle of feet as the train screeches to a halt. The lens crashes violently into one of the silver poles in the aisle.

All eyes move to the damaged equipment on the floor. "What a shame," they must think, "such a beautiful camera, and so expensive!" They have no idea.

I step out onto the congested Times Square platform, avoiding any eye contact as the crowd of commuters shuffle in and out.

I suspect someone will find out that he isn't sleeping by Chambers Street.

They always say, "if looks could kill." If only they knew.

Ballerina

by Luiza Guimarães

Lucy walked fast down the streets of London, forgetting to put her back straight as a proper ballerina would. She was looking down and trying to hold back her tears, desperately wanting to forget the last hour's talk. But the conversation with her ballet teacher kept repeating itself in her mind like a mantra.

"You want me to be honest? Ok, I'll be honest with you," said her teacher, Mrs. Raven, as calmly as if she was talking to a stubborn child, even though Lucy had just turned eighteen. "You don't look like a ballerina."

Lucy had prepared herself the whole week for this day, the day when she would face that woman and ask her why, after sixteen years of dancing at her school, of giving every fiber of her being to the classes and rehearsals and choreographies, she had never stepped on a proper stage.

But when she received the answer all her will vanished and she realized how foolish she had been for trusting Mrs. Raven for her whole life.

"I know," was everything she found the strength to reply. She clenched her fists.

"And you never will. You are fat, your bones are large, and you are way too tall."

Mrs. Raven had a look of pity in her eyes, as if it was hurting her more to say the words than for Lucy to hear them.

The girl looked down, thinking about the six pounds she had lost in the last four-and-a-half months and how her teacher seemed to have ignored the changes in her body. She always knew she was fat for a ballerina, but she had been working hard to change that reality and in the recent months she had felt like she had achieved something . . . or at least she thought she had.

"That will never change. It is your natural build. You may try to lose as many pounds as you wish, you will always be too fat to dance in a *tutu*."

Lucy was wordless.

"I don't want to expose you by putting you on a stage beside all those girls who are not only much better than you in dance, but thinner too." The teacher had put one hand on Lucy's shoulder.

The ballerina felt a lump in her throat and her eyes dangerously wet, most of all, she just wanted to get rid of her teacher's stupid hand.

"But . . . I thought . . . you always told us when we were children that if we put enough effort into ballet, you would see it, and take it into account when you were choosing the ones who were going to dance at the performances. I've been working so hard! Why don't you give me one chance? I can prove I'm good!"

The teacher sighed and dropped her hand.

"Lucy, you don't fit in. If you like to come to my school and have some classes, I'm fine with it, but if you are expecting me to choose you for some dance performance in a proper theater! Moreover, beside my best ballerinas! I suggest you go find a new dance style for yourself. You will never be good at classical. Fix that in your mind. Sometimes effort is not enough. Try to see my side, I own this place, I must build a good reputation for my school."

And you don't want me to ruin it. I got it.

She hadn't said that last part out loud. Actually, she hadn't managed to say anything else, as she had feared she was going to start crying any minute. Somehow, she managed to say a proper goodbye to Mrs. Raven and leave the school with a good part of her dignity intact.

And here she was, walking around Covent Garden with no specific destination in mind, trying hard not to cry. She couldn't cry on the street; it would call too much attention towards her and that was the last thing she wanted.

She thought of her home. No, she couldn't go home as well. Her mother would be there, and she knew very well what the woman would say,

"My darling, you should give up ballet. It is not for you. I know you love

to dance, so why don't you go for something more exciting? Like jazz or contemporary? Maybe even hip hop?"

Even her mother thought that she wasn't cut out for classical dancing.

If Lucy arrived at home crying, then it was guaranteed that her mother would stop paying for the ballet classes and she couldn't visualize her life without ballet.

The girl saw the white Covent Garden market at some distance. It was crowded with tourists. She couldn't cry in there as well.

There are so many places where one can't cry.

She inhaled the fresh air and kept walking, crossing the market while trying to calm herself down and face the situation rationally.

She had been told that her biggest dream would never come true. What could she do now? She was eighteen years old already. Sixteen years of ballet! Sixteen long years of trying to shape her body into unnatural forms that would be fitting for dance. Sixteen years of seeing all her friends being casted in wonderful performances—*The Nutcracker, Le Corsaire, Don Quixote* . . . Every year Mrs. Raven dismissed her with a *"maybe next year."*

I'm so stupid!

It was time for her to wake up from that childish dream she had been living-in ever since she started to dance. She had had an absurdly high level of patience with Mrs. Raven, but now enough was enough.

Lucy had always believed in the words she had heard all her childhood, that people who worked hard could get what they wanted. In school, that had always been proven right. Why wasn't it working now?

She looked to the gray sky as if asking for some answers.

Lucy had crossed the whole market and hadn't even realized that. She looked up to find where her legs had unconsciously taken her—to the bronze ballerina statue resting on her high stool and adjusting her left pointe shoe.

The Covent Garden Ballerina.

Lucy couldn't hold back her tears anymore. She looked from the statue to the magnificent entrance of the Royal Opera House. She started sobbing.

When she was only twelve, she had believed that one day she would be dancing at the Royal Ballet. As she got older, she had realized that she would never be a professional dancer. Dancing for her was a pleasure and making it her job would only ruin her feelings toward it.

At least that was what my mother helped me realize.

She walked towards the ballerina statue and sat beside it, letting her tears flow without ceremony. She rested her head against the right bronze leg, trying to absorb some of the strength and tranquility that came from that statue.

She looked at the Opera House and thought she might have heard some music.

They are probably rehearsing something.

But Lucy knew that the classrooms were too distant for her to be listening to anything. It was only her imagination playing tricks on her. Again.

"Need some help, down there?" said a metallic voice from above Lucy's head. The girl tried to dry her tears while she looked for the one who was speaking.

"I'm fine, thank . . ." She stopped talking. No one was there, only her.

Your imagination again, Lucy . . .

"Well, you look quite sad, you know?"

Lucy frowned. She was sure she had heard a voice coming from above her head.

"Where . . . where are . . . you?"

I must be looking so pathetic.

"Why, I'm right here! Are you blind or something?"

Lucy looked above and saw the face of the statue looking at her with concern. Her eyes popped open.

"Ah! Now you see me," said the bronze ballerina with her frozen smile. "What is quite interesting, if you think about it, is that you are resting your cheek very comfortably against my leg. Yet . . ."

Lucy removed her face at once, feeling kind of guilty.

"I'm sorry."

Am I excusing myself to a statue?

"Don't you worry about that, darling, you would be surprised by the number of people who lay against me every day!"

She sounded as one would when waving off a meaningless subject. However, she didn't make any move, not even her mouth changed when she spoke. The ballerina was still frozen in the position she had been made, tying up her point shoe, a faint smile on her lips.

"But anyway, as I was saying . . . Won't you tell me what's happened?"

Lucy dried her tears and rolled her eyes, deciding there was nothing to lose in sharing her feelings with a statue.

"It's my ballet teacher . . ."

"Oh! It always is!"

Always? How many ballerinas had she sat beside and heard their feelings?

"Well . . . She said I will never be good at classical, that I should choose another style if I wanted to keep dancing. She said that I don't look like a ballerina, and that I am not fit for ballet."

"Yes . . ." said the bronze ballerina, her eyes kind.

"The thing is . . . I can't live without ballet. I can't dance in any other style."

"And why is that?"

The girl sighed. She was tired of explaining *why*.

"Ballet, it's just . . . ballet! A ballerina is strong, but delicate at the same time. You work hard and when you see the results . . . It is wonderful!"

The statue looked skeptical.

"So are the other dances. For me, you just sound prejudiced."

Lucy crossed her arms.

"I thought that you, of all people, would understand me, you are a ballerina!"

The bronze ballerina turned her head towards Lucy, or at least tried to.

"No, I'm not a ballerina, I'm the statue of a ballerina."

The girl shrugged her shoulders.

"It's the same thing."

The statue gave a snort that could be mistaken for a laugh.

"Well, my darling, it is not! Look at me, what is the main difference between me and, let's say, you—a real ballerina?"

Lucy felt a small hint of pride when the bronze statue called her a real ballerina. But she couldn't see any difference between them, only that the statue was thinner and prettier.

"Uh . . . I don't know . . ."

"I can't move!" shouted the Covent Garden Ballerina, as if it was something obvious.

Lucy frowned.

"Statues don't move."

"Statues don't talk either and yet here we are!"

The girl had to give her that.

"Now, tell me, why ballet?" If she could move, she would probably be putting her hands on her waist right now, but instead, she just looked at her with a challenging expression. "What does ballet have that pulls you so much?"

Lucy gave a hard thought this time. She remembered her feelings when she had first dressed in her pointe shoes. She remembered the joy she felt every time she jumped in a *grand jeté*. She smiled and gave a childish answer.

"It is the only dance where you can fly!"

The ballerina frowned, confused by the answer, but she accepted it.

"Very well."

Lucy smiled at the statue and then looked at the Royal Ballet once more, and her brief good mood disappeared. She went quiet for a while, picturing a future as a professional dancer, a future that never would happen. She sobbed and let her head fall against the ballerina's leg once more.

"I just . . . I feel like I've thrown away a whole life of effort. I will never be anything more than I already am. I will never dance *The Swan Lake* or *La Bayadère*. And I am not even saying a solo, just a small part in the back of the *corps du ballet* would have been enough!"

The girl realized her voice had risen a bit.

"I'm sorry . . . I'm shouting at you."

The statue gave her a small, reassuring smile.

"You do sound outraged."

"And I am!" Lucy threw her hands in the air and sighed. "Don't I have a point?"

The bronze ballerina looked at her with the air of a person who knows a lot more than they actually have the desire to share.

"What?" asked the girl.

"Do you want me to be honest with you?"

Lucy hesitated, hearing that same question for the second time that day. But she crossed her arms and braved on.

"Yes, please."

A noise came from the back stairs of the Opera House and Lucy saw a group of dancers getting out, talking excitedly among themselves, and carrying large and heavy bags on their shoulders.

Those dancers were probably her age and they looked so happy.

"Look at them," said the ballerina.

"Who?" She played the ignorant.

"You know who! Those dancers over there."

Reluctantly, Lucy turned her head back toward the group. She saw them walking away, to the Covent Garden Market.

"What about them?"

"They come to rehearse every single day. They are a part of the company."

"Lucky them."

"Yes, lucky them. Every single day I watch them leave their rehearsal, sometimes happy, sometimes tired, sometimes hurt . . . And here I am, sitting on this stool since I was made, resting, waiting for my turn to dance . . . And you know what? It never came."

Of course, it never came! You are a statue! You can't move, you can't dance . . .

But at the very moment she thought this, Lucy realized what the ballerina was trying to tell her.

"I guess I am not fit for ballet either."

"And yet you look just like a proper ballerina would," finished Lucy.

The statue smiled.

"Yes. My darling, you and I are the same. I have the body; you have the movement. I would never be successful in any other dance style; I would just remain sitting here. You, on the other hand, could choose any other style and be the best at it. But not in ballet. Ballet is a tricky thing—the most difficult and yet the most beautiful form of art. At least from my point of view."

Lucy couldn't agree more.

The girl sighed.

"So, you're telling me that I should focus on other types of dance." She had heard that from many people already, it wasn't any news. Plus, it still reinforced what Mrs. Raven and her mom had always told her: too big for ballet.

But the bronze ballerina just lifted her brows and exclaimed.

"Why, no! I am telling you to live and be happy. To make your own choices. If you are a ballerina, you are a ballerina. That cannot change! I know that myself, trust me!"

Lucy lifted her head and dried a few remaining tears from her face. She frowned.

"But how ... ?"

"Just promise me one thing, would you? Don't let another ballet teacher ruin another ballerina's love for dance. I have already seen too much of this since I was made."

The girl nodded, still trying to figure out the meaning of the statue's last words.

"You said ... be happy ... I'm sorry but that is not very strong advice ..."

The Covent Garden Ballerina answered nothing. Lucy checked her face and saw only the peaceful expression that the artist had sculpted so many years ago.

Am I getting insane? Did I just have a chat with a statue?

Whether the metal creature beside her had spoken or not, Lucy couldn't deny that she had received precious advice.

She was eighteen years old. It was more than time for her to let go of her childish beliefs. "Live and be happy," the ballerina had said. That was precisely what she would do.

Now she could see it. She had almost lost the pleasure she always felt in dance, all that excitement she used to feel when walking on the tip of her toes in pointe shoes, or the flying sensation she used to have when she jumped in a *grand jeté*—everything had been threatened in the last few years by the shadow of Mrs. Raven above her.

Lucy had wanted her approval so badly that she was losing her love for the art of ballet.

That was the attitude of a child.

A whole new world of choices had opened in front of her, and she would take the best out of it.

It didn't matter if she was fat, or tall, or didn't look like a proper ballerina. She would find a place that could take her for who she was and, if that place didn't exist, then she would create one herself.

She smiled at the last thought. Yes, she could create a new place where people like her would be accepted. Actually, it was more than time for her to choose a career, wasn't it?

It's probably going to be a lot more difficult than I am thinking of right now.

But she didn't care; it was a challenge that she was willing to take.

Lucy smiled and walked to the Covent Garden Market, following the same way as the group of dancers she had seen before. She stopped half-way and looked back at the Covent Garden Ballerina.

"Thanks."

She said and, for one moment, she thought she had seen the illusion of a movement, as if the statue was acknowledging her with her head.

Ache

by Camille Daniels

I starve to speak,

Words escape my hands out of my fingertips,

They take up space in my mind,

Stuck at the tip of my tongue,

Barricaded by my closed mouth,

Thoughts and feelings come to me,

Images never do,

Yet the urge to grab a pen,

The urge to find paper,

Come to me like prepared messages,

Waiting for me to send them out into the world,

But I don't,

Instead, I sit,

I think and contemplate my fears.

Fears of rejection,

Fears of being ignored,

And dread the fear of criticism,

Or simply being forgotten,

I ache,

The pain of it all swirls around in my soul,

Knowing that I should do more,

But instead, I don't,

For some wonder, "Why not speak?"

And to them I say, "You are not me"

Yet the words still remain, forming, building off the feelings that are in existence waiting for me to do something,

To say something, to write something.

A Piazza in Sicily

by Nicolina Barone

It was a day the boys had nothing planned. Mateo and Luca had Sunday dinner with their families so I knew the extent of my afternoon would be free. The way of life in Italy is a way that can never be replicated back in the United States. It's a place with nowhere to go and nothing to do and it's simply okay. It's okay to exist and to drink your morning coffee for three hours among your friends. You realize that it is okay to move slowly because here, the world won't continue moving without you. You can move to your own rhythm.

Sundays were a day of rest and God. I knew the 2:00 p.m. mass was getting out soon and that there would be someone to paint. One face in the crowd would speak to me. Brushes, paint, and my canvas were all I needed. My thumb brushed over the initials written on my palette, F. M., Francesca Marino, my mom's maiden name before she took my father's last name, Carlentini. When I first got accepted into the Florence Academy of Art, she placed it on my bed under the opened envelope. She was too anxious to have waited for me to get home from school that day to find out if I would be leaving her.

I began getting myself situated. I sat and I waited. I knew there was a chance no one would speak to me, that just like my project, it was a possibility my talents were not salvageable. Then the doors were pushed open, voices grew louder, and the piazza was filled with the Holy Spirit. Women with their shoulders covered by shawls, the younger ones slowly slipping them off as they reached the bottom of the church's steps. Nonnas hurrying home to start the sauce, cousins chasing one another, and mothers talking to sisters. It was a sight to see, a sight to wish for, a sight to make you miss home. I did it to myself, that I know, I left my family, I hear your remarks, even though they are just being said in your mind.

A man began walking through the crowd, his white cane leading the way for him. I hadn't realized until he almost bumped into someone who rolled their eyes at him that the cane wasn't for stability. I slowly approached him and asked him politely if I could paint a picture of him.

He laughed, almost immediately, a low, raspy laugh. Like he hadn't laughed in so long his vocal cords were being cleaned off by the use of them now. He sat then, on the fountain not too far away, and I placed my hand behind his back, letting him know there was water behind him. He took his sunglasses off, holding them in front of him, I grabbed them and placed them carefully in my backpack. He had these milky blue eyes, barely a pupil in sight. He spoke with a raspy Italian accent, one I imagined my grandfather might have had.

"Why are you painting me?" he asked then.

I hesitated for a moment, "Um sir, what do you mean?"

"I've never seen color before, but I can be sure that I am not something to be painted," he said quietly.

I had the rough outline done at this point, the rough edges and lines, his pointed nose, his crooked smile, and then I realized I would need to verbalize not only what I was painting, but the colors I was using. I didn't paint perfect sketches or replicas of their faces. Their faces were on the canvas of course, but it was abstract. Shapes and lines and splotches of color meshing together, speaking to who they were more than what they looked like. Parts could appear like blobs, the colors mixing behind his face and within it. The reds mixing with the orange, his hair turning darker the more paint I added to the mix. He was color. He was the embodiment of life and struggle and grief and laughter. To be born different and have it deemed wrong. There were smudges and smears of red and orange spilling down the canvas. I told him that I would tell him about the color I had made. A color that's hot and loud. I asked if he had ever loved before and he gently nodded his head.

I told him it was the color of air you felt around you when your arms were around that person, when your lips met. The heat between the two of you. The way their hands felt gripping your body. That close wasn't close enough. Like it was the last time you could ever feel their touch. The addiction, the pain, the desire. I told him it was also the color you saw when that person was found under the covers with another man. Spilling, draining, out of your ears. Oozing down your face, dripping slowly down, landing on the left side of your chest, burning a hole straight through it. The color of your voice when you saw them. A voice that didn't belong to you, but someone you assumed lived deep inside of you. Simply waiting for the chance to consume you and cloud your judgment.

His eyelids seemed heavy then, as he blinked a time or two, and they began to shut. The description causing a shudder. I let him sit with it. Let him feel the way I had felt all these years about the world. Allow him to perceive color through my eyes. I continued painting, thinking that his eyes closed would fit the painting better. The representation of a life he lived but never once saw. The beige around him wanting to consume him, pixelating his hair in conjunction with his part. The beige attempted to take him away, to fade him from our vision, the way we were more than faded from his. But he fought, the red on his cheeks peeked through, behind his ears, speckles on his neck. A red of passion, of war, of fighting for a life that was never really accepting of him.

The trance was halted then, with the sound of a familiar voice. Looking down at my hands, forgetting the very color of my palms. My fingertips stained with shades of pink, red, yellow, and orange. My grandmother's old promise ring stained. And I still never figured out if it was from the rust of never taking it off or the paint.

"What are you doing here?" Galileo asked. He gazed keenly then at my work. He was dressed in a light green button-up with khakis and leather shoes. The piazza had cleared up. I hadn't realized how quiet it was until his voice was quite literally the only thing I could hear. He must have just left mass with his family. I wondered how long he had been there for, waiting, watching.

"I needed to paint. To get out of my rut," I said, finally swinging around to look at him.

He knew to never disturb a creative in their trance. That the vision could forever be lost. That if it wasn't done in that moment, at that time, it could never end up this original way again. It was an unspoken language between artists. Realizing it too, he slowly backed away about five feet or so behind me. I couldn't even hear him breathing.

"Continue please. Go on."

I went on layering my paint. Building up the paint and the color. I practiced the technique our teacher taught us. Wet paint over wet paint, mixing them, creating these colors and mixtures to embody the very essence of this man. I had finished applying the lean layers, I made sure to add fatter layers on top of the colors I liked and wanted to stay. To ensure that cracking would be avoided. I loved it, and Galileo did too. The moment I took a step back to see it from a different perspective, to get it out from directly in front of my eyes, he began to clap. Realizing what was happening the man began to clap with him.

"I may not be able to see it dear, but I feel your talent. The other senses have to overcompensate for the ones that don't work," He spoke softly, with a warmth in his tone. "I can feel that you are an artist. In your blood."

functioning again.
by Hannah Penn

My mother says that my bones
will become one the longer
I remain still.
As impossible as it is,
and I tell her that,
I find myself longing for movement.

I wish to move like the trees,
and elegantly glide across a pond
like the birds I watch from the window.
When I stand from my chair,
my bones creak like the
trunks of trees in the wind,
and I remember why humans
are not made to remain stagnant.

I pull on sneakers and
feel the welcoming ache in my joints.
My body groans and cracks,
but I cannot remain still anymore.
Movement does not come with ease;
not when the world is motionless.
It will take time, but this is a start.

Like Real People Do

by Katie Schwab

Halloween in suburbia was an event if there ever was one.

Cul-de-sacs were swarmed with sugar-high children holding pillowcases and margarita-drunk parents holding jackets, while houses that all looked the same donned cheap Party City string lights around their doors and cotton spider webs in their bushes.

Halloween was Hana's favorite of the calendar holidays. She'd worn the same costume every year for the last several decades, updating materials and application methods whenever time made it necessary. It amused her endlessly: an inside joke meant only for herself, though. It was also the one night a year that allowed her to be completely transparent, the one night where she didn't have to be a lie.

If you walked far enough down the street, past the family homes and the chaos of trick-or-treaters, to where festivities happened inside rather than out, you'd start to hear the playful screams of college drinkers, the thump of a bass line traveling through pavement and under shoes.

Hana paused in the walkway in front of the dead-grassed and paint-chipped AEπ house. Last year, she'd attended the party at Theta Chi—a historically dull thirty-first. Tonight, something inside her tingled; an odd sensation for her, as she hardly felt anything these days. Briefly, she thought of phantom heartbeats and the intangible memory of what that must have felt like. The racing nature of a pulse. Admittedly, it had been a long time.

Anticipation.

Hana pushed open the front door.

Wading through mingling clouds of tobacco and marijuana, she followed the hallway past the made-up faces of her classmates: a Bambi, a Batman, a Barack. Three different black cats—the tallest of the clowder a rather cute Magical Mr. Mistoffelees. Hana recognized her from her Anatomy lecture.

She found the kitchen. If she was going to treat herself to a night of observing, she'd need to be buzzed enough to find it entertaining. Since

47

the refrigerator was blocked by a lip-locked pair of Wiggles, Hana stole an unopened and sweating PBR from the counter and went out back. There was a pool outside with a dozen half-naked twenty-somethings playing chicken, splashing and squealing with the gleeful carelessness of being young and alive. She wondered if any of them felt cold, or just didn't care. Not that she had a sense of temperature anymore, but the app on her phone suggested rain later. Claiming an open chair on the lawn, she took a seat and opened her beer.

"Do people still dress up as mummies these days?"

Hana turned in her chair. Behind her was a girl, tall and wiry, draped in black velvet and lace, holding a red plastic cup. The scuffed toes of two Mary Janes peeked out from the bottom trim of her cloak. She was ghostly pale—a shocking contrast to her black hair, dark painted eyelids and blood-red lipstick, an intentional trail drawn outside the lines and down the left corner of her mouth. A vampire.

Hana raised a brow. "Excuse me?"

"Seems like costumes are made with fewer materials each year," Vampire girl smiled, displaying two stake-sharp fangs. "We're the only two people I've seen tonight dressed appropriately for the weather."

Hana took in the full sight of her, a brief and small allowance. She smiled back.

"You're one to talk. I figured people stopped dressing up as vampires after Twilight."

Vampira scoffed with a dramatic eyeroll—from where she sat, Hana couldn't quite make out their color.

"Nothing more than terribly inaccurate fanfiction. I've never once glittered in the sunlight."

Hana laughed. "Right. I'm Hana."

"Minnie."

"Shouldn't you be dressed as a mouse, then?"

"Ha-ha. Your lack of originality is disappointing."

"Apologies."

"It's alright." There were a few abandoned chairs scattered on the grass, and Minnie moved to grab one, dragging it over and planting it next Hana's. She sat gracefully, her cape billowing under her, and set her cup down at her feet. "You can't help your rotted brain."

There was a brief commotion, as two frat brothers wrestled on the lawn while peers with smartphones egged them on. The larger of the two—the one clearly winning—picked up the other by the hips and charged at full speed toward the pool. Nearby, a group of girls jumped, shrieking out of the way, while Hana blinked coolly at Minnie's knocked over cup.

"Hey, your drink—"

"Don't mind it," Minnie said, kicking the cup away with her foot. "There was never anything in it."

"Did you want—" Hana gestured in the direction of the kitchen.

"I don't drink."

"Oh. Why not?"

Minnie shrugged. "I don't have the appetite for alcohol."

"Nothing wrong with that. Why carry around an empty cup, though?"

Minnie smiled again, all glinting, pointed teeth. "It's fun. Looking the part of something you don't belong to."

Gold—Minnie's eyes were gold. Hana couldn't help but stare back at her with quiet curiosity.

"You don't come to a lot of these things, do you?"

"Something tells me you don't either," Minnie said.

Hana opened her mouth, but nothing came out. Abruptly, she stood, turning herself toward the house in sudden awkwardness, knowing that she couldn't blush but feeling like she was doing it anyway.

"Did you want to grab some water at least? I—"

When she turned back around, Minnie's chair was empty.

For the next half hour, Hana wandered through the house feeling as if she might have hallucinated. Was that possible? More so, she felt disappointment. It wasn't every day she had interesting conversations with cute, mysterious girls dressed as monsters popping in and out of nowhere. Or at all.

She didn't form relationships—not that talking to a girl for four minutes constituted a relationship, *get a grip, darling*. Her life was complicated enough being undead. She wasn't a ghost, like she'd first wondered; when she held her hands to a wall, she answered to physics, palms met with resistance instead of phasing through. She knew enough tales of hubris not to call herself a god, and yet she existed, undecayed, her body frozen in time everywhere, apart from her mind. After she fled England, Hana understood that her mind and its elastic memory might be her greatest defense. She would spend eternity, alone—safe—learning the world, until the long-awaited day where, finally, there existed a way of ending it all.

But relationships meant closeness. They meant expectations, revelations of secrets, of (arguably worse) truths, and, usually, they meant another transfer, another school. Even in life Hana had an unfortunate affinity for telling the truth: how do you think she ended up dead?

Somehow, she always managed to say too much despite her greatest attempts at keeping herself from others, no matter how . . . *intriguing* she may find them. It was obvious enough to assume people preferred their girlfriends, you know, alive.

Hana may have traded safety for solitude, but a trade was still a choice; it didn't make her any less lonely.

She only lasted another ten minutes before leaving the party, slipping out the way she slipped in. It was a nice enough night, no rain yet. She'd take a walk.

Hana walked far out of the neighborhoods, past the groups of trick-or-treaters thinning as the night pressed on. She walked through the college until she reached the wooded arboretum that stretched along the north perimeter of campus. During the day, students sat out on the grass to study or picnic, taking advantage of the fresh air before the chill of winter inevitably chased them toward the library.

At night, there was no one. The woods looked as sinister as they probably felt. It was dark—threateningly, hauntingly dark. Lampposts existed few and far between; even still, they flickered too dimly to provide anyone passing through with the safety of sight.

Hana was not scared—she *wasn't*. She had no reason to be, not here. Even so, what was there to fear if death was no longer on the table? Paranoia was an emotion for girls who could sweat.

She dug out her little wireless headphones, stuffed and trapped somewhere under shredded layers of gauze.

There were pockets of beauty in infinity, Hana had to admit; in living centuries longer than you were meant to, you became a witness to the brilliance of evolution, of the bullet train that was technology. Time was simultaneously nonexistent and never-ending; in a blink, she could listen to operas through her telephone.

She queued her favorite playlist (Wolfgang had nothing on Taylor Swift) and kept along the paved trail as the darkness devoured her.

Then, Hana sensed something. No, *saw* something—a quick flash in her peripheral. She threw a lazy glance over her shoulder, and when she saw nothing, she let it go. The first time, anyway.

It happened again, and then a third time. Hana knew she was being followed. She felt no panic, only deep annoyance. Sighing, she kept her face forward. There was what looked like the only functioning lamppost in this stretch of the woods six meters down the path. She waited until she was fully veiled by light, and then, in a swift, singular movement, she whirled around, ripping a low-hanging branch from off the path and—

Hana froze.

It was Vampire Girl. Minnie.

"Christ," Minnie huffed, golden eyes zeroed in on the sharp stake in Hana's hand, raised and aimed closely at her chest. "Do you mind?"

Hana frowned, dropping the branch. She took out an earbud.

"Have you been following me?"

"No, actually," Minnie said, smirking now that she wasn't about to be shanked.

Hana furrowed her brow. "Why are you out here?"

"I could ask you the same thing. What are *you* doing."

Hana blinked. "Walking."

"Hmm," Minnie hummed, nodding. Her red lips pulled into a taut, wide smile. "Very like-minded of us."

Hana had that un-flushed, flushed feeling again. She shifted, awkward under Minnie's stare. Now, both standing, Minnie was several inches taller, her pale skin glowing soft yellow under the artificial light. It had been so long since Hana was the object of someone's extended attention.

"It's not safe for you to be here by yourself," she said.

Minnie's eyebrow quirked. "And not for you?"

Hana shrugged. With the toe of her boot, she kicked weakly at the branch on the pavement. "I had my stake."

Minnie laughed.

Oh, Hana thought to herself. *What an elegant sound.*

Ungracefully, she stuck her hands again down the pockets of her gauze-wrapped jeans. She could feel Minnie's eyes following her movements.

"Where did you go earlier?" Hana asked.

"Hmm?"

"At the party. I was going to ask—" Hana cleared her throat. "But you disappeared."

It was Minnie's turn to play coy. "I got hungry, so I left." She put her hands into the pockets of her cloak, mirroring Hana. "Wasn't really my scene, anyway."

"Why did you go then?"

"I was invited."

It was then that Hana did what she shouldn't have: she broke one of her sacred, dumb rules, because even as a dead girl, she was foolish.

She asked Minnie a question about herself: "So, what is your scene?"

Minnie's grin spread so incredibly wide, her fangs out on full display. She took Hana by the hand; her fingers were rough and cold like carved stone, yet Hana echoed warmth. "Here. I'll show you."

Like beasts of the night, they crept through the woods, embracing darkness like a friend, passing trees so tall they fused with the sky, picking flowers that had yet to die late in the season, braiding them into crowns. They ventured off the path and down onto the bank of the creek that flowed through the area. Hana taught Minnie how to skip rocks—a skill she picked up thirty years ago in Montana—and in turn, Minnie showed Hana how to speak to friends with wings.

"Watch this," Minnie said, stretching her arms into a T. She let out a shrill whistle, so high-pitched it stung Hana's eardrums, except, the ringing wasn't coming from her ears; a dozen winged creatures appeared out of the shadows surrounding them, swarming, before landing comfortably along Minnie's arms.

Hana stared at her, aghast. Then, deep-bellied laughter. "*Bats?* A bit on the nose, don't you think?"

As they crossed the stream, a niggling thought stayed with her, unplaceable and unnamable; she tucked it away, for now.

Soon, a break in the trees opened to a wide, open field. Tall grass swayed, yellowed in the face of a California November, with hay barrels scattered, unorganized, abandoned. The fields belonged to the school, though Hana had never been this far along the perimeter before. She figured most students probably hadn't. Except, it appeared, Minnie.

Minnie spun to face her, another smirk on her lips; Hana began to wonder if this was her default setting.

"Has anyone ever told you," Minnie asked, "what you do in an open field at midnight?"

"No. What do you do?"

Minnie crept closer. Hana tensed, fighting every instinct her body carried to run as Minnie placed her hands gently on her hip as she leaned in to whisper, "You dance under the stars."

Then, the cool weight of her vanished. Hana hadn't realized she'd closed her eyes, but when she opened them, Minnie was nearly halfway across the field, her cloak flapping wildly behind her.

For a moment, Hana couldn't move, her boots frozen in magical mud. Because there it was again: a rhythmic rush, in the edgeless shape of a memory, of a wildly beating heart—bereft of touch, of closeness, of curiosity. Hana watched her run, in pure, terrifying wonder. And then she followed.

She ran with the gift of immortal lungs until they collided, Minnie screaming in delight with the bats.

As it was, Hana learned a new, yet ageless truth: it was a night for dancing.

Hana lent Minnie an earbud and their worlds swirled with Irish crooning. They danced—fiercely, with no patience for elegance, only freedom. They danced—even as the rain joined in. They didn't care; they kept dancing. Hana lost streamers and the ends of Minnie's cloak grew caked with mud; still, they kept dancing. They linked elbows and skipped in circles, undoubtedly looking like a strange, ridiculous pair. It was the first night Hana had felt truly, wondrously, alive since the last time her life was simply, beautifully that: her *life*. She missed it with a fire inside her. For a moment, white and hot, she was envious of mortality; she yearned for the opportunity to dance with someone until only brittle bones and graying hearts could stop them.

Hana's phone died; the music stopped, and so did they. Without their permission, the sky had gone from black to purple. Morning was coming.

They stood facing one another, drenched head to toe. The rain danced without them.

Despite the ghoulish way her makeup bled down her face, Minnie remained frustratingly beautiful; she inched closer and closer.

Their lips were inches apart when Hana ripped herself away.

Panicked, she staggered hazardously toward the tree line. Toward campus, the houses, the party, anonymity—*safety*.

She was embarrassed. Ashamed. Angry with her circumstances in a way she wouldn't normally allow herself to be, as anger was an exhausting human affliction. Yet the thought only enraged her more:

she wasn't *human anymore. Why,* she pleaded, *must she be plagued with all these emotions without a soul to attach them to?*

"What year did you die?" asked Minnie.

Hana froze, startled for a moment by the sound within the silence she'd created, before turning hotly.

"I'm—what?"

"What year did you die?" Minnie repeated patiently. She walked slowly, feigning a casualty that conflicted with the question.

Hana stared with wild eyes.

"How—"

"How?" Another step. "It takes a monster to know a monster, Hana."

Minnie took small, careful steps, as if approaching an animal on the brink of fleeing. She smiled, not unkindly, as she reached for Hana's wrist, tenderly running her thumb where a pulse once drummed.

"That," Minnie continued, "and the fact that I can't smell your blood. It ran cold some time ago, didn't it?"

Holy shit.

"1891." The confession fell from Hana's lips. "At Oxford. I was twenty."

She had never said that out loud before.

Minnie smiled and nodded, as if proud; there was comradery in the shared survival of centuries.

"Middle Ages. 1317, to be specific—Glasgow. Though I was born in Normandy."

"Incredible," Hana breathed. "I can hardly believe it."

"What," Minnie said. The rain softened as the sky lightened. She tucked a wet strand of hair behind Hana's ear. It felt so nice. "You didn't think you were the only one, did you?"

"Well, no. But . . . I've never—"

Flashes of the night bombarded her: the fangs, the bats. *Smelling blood.* Hana cackled. "You dressed up as a vampire for Halloween."

"Yes, darling. We can unpack the irony of us hiding in plain sight later, but, please," Minnie leaned down again. Hana didn't feel breath against her lips, but she no longer expected to; now, neither needed to pretend. "Kiss me before the sun comes up."

And she did.

They kissed and kissed in soaked clothes and mud, until it grew too light for Minnie to risk being out of the shade. She stole a final kiss before whispering against the skin of Hana's cheekbone, "Tomorrow. Meet me here, at midnight."

As she watched Minnie's frame disappear through the woods, Hana held fingers to her bitten mouth, completely undone—in wrappings, in stupor. She couldn't fight her smile. Wouldn't, perhaps, ever again.

For, after all this time, she just might get to have something, like real people do.

Acatalepsy.

by Hannah Penn

Each night she lies awake.
Pondering an existence
without the infinitely stretching galaxy
that swirls within her mind.
Or perhaps,
she ponders existence itself.

For each night she observes
the galaxy seemingly just out of reach
with stars that ripple throughout the dark sky.
All the while, the spinning disarray
behind starlit eyes continuously pounds
against the retention wall of logic.

It is in these moments
that she ponders existence.
What it would be like to burn like a star.
Free from thought.
Or the thought that we know.
Free from this existence.

The Last Interface
by Shea Dunlop

Jackie can see a glimpse of the outside world through the window in Sam's room. Lately, her friends have been taking turns crossing her perfectly programmed lawn to sit on her auto-generated front porch and gaze out at the wall of pixels. All of their interfaces have gone dark by now, shutting down one by one. Jackie's view is the only one left in the neighborhood.

Jackie's player is a creature of habit. He usually powers up his computer as he gets ready for school, around 7 a.m. This morning is no different.

The front-facing wall of Jackie's second-floor bedroom blinks out of existence. It's replaced by Sam's tousled brown hair and bright blue eyes peering in at her through square glasses. She hops out of bed and stretches, offering him a "Good morning!" she knows he won't understand.

Nevertheless, he smiles. "*Gurb nargin* to you, too, Jackie!"

His eyes flick to the corner of his screen, checking her bank account. She makes her bed, then stands by the door, waiting for him to click the "Daily Routine" button, as he always does on school days.

Jackie's routine allows her to Free Roam in the neighborhood. Her routine also includes "going to work." But with no player watching, she doesn't actually have to do anything to earn money, it just appears in her bank account at the end of the day.

"Work hard today, okay?" he says, setting her on her course and gathering up his pre-algebra homework from the night before. "I know you've been wanting me to customize the porch."

Sam had noticed the porch attracting the neighbors and finally got the hint that the two rock-hard wicker chairs from the Basic Porch expansion weren't cutting it.

Jackie heads downstairs to make breakfast, keeping an eye on the interface as her hallway and kitchen walls disappear.

Sam's desk sits opposite the window in his narrow bedroom, allowing Jackie and her friends to watch the leaves change on the old oak tree and track the clouds across the sky.

Though she can't see it, she knows the door is to the left of her view, because that's where he comes and goes from. The bunk bed he's outgrown is to the right of her view. He grumbles about it sometimes in the morning when he wakes up with a sore neck, but he won't tell his dad.

Jackie knows money doesn't just appear at the end of a workday in the outside world.

Even at age 11, Sam understands this, too.

"I'm cooooold," he says to her, shoving his folders into his backpack. "Dad's keeping the heat down again."

Jackie cracks an egg into a pan, watching him fumble with the broken zipper. "I'm sorry," she responds. "I wish there was something I could do!"

He glances over at her. "Eggs this morning?"

There's a knock on Sam's door. "Yeah?" He calls out, ducking out of her view to rifle through his dresser.

Jackie hears Sam's dad come in, the old door creaking on its hinges.

"Happy Monday! Talking to Jackie again?" Dad asks, swinging his head into her view. Jackie flips her egg with a flick of her wrist, catching his grin through the side of her kitchen.

"No!" Sam lies. "Just talking."

"Uh-huh," Dad chuckles. "Hey, kiddo, Christmas is coming up . . . How about that new version of FML?"

Jackie freezes, listening.

"Daaaaad, it's not FML, that means 'frick my life!'" Laughing at his dad's accidental swearing, Sam corrects him, "It's FNL, *Friendly Neighborhood Living*."

"Of course, of course," Dad confirms. "How about it, huh?"

Jackie doesn't move. She's been dreading this. All of Sam's friends, the kids who once designed her neighbors' houses, had moved on. Her whole neighborhood, their shared server, had FNL 2.0 to blame for the dark static interfaces in every yard.

Once Sam stopped playing . . . well, she didn't know what would happen. Would her interface go dark, leaving them all trapped in stasis? Would they cease to exist altogether? Her next-door neighbor, Marvin, had some wild theories, but they'd all been just theories until now.

"See?" Dad taps the monitor. "Jackie froze up. I bet the new version is smooth as butter." Jackie shakes herself and quickly plates her egg. She can't afford to slip up like that again.

"That would be pretty sick . . ." Sam thinks for a moment. Jackie's heart races.

"I don't know, Dad," Sam turns to look out the window. "It's really expensive."

Dad joins him, placing a hand on his shoulder. Jackie watches them with bated breath.

"I'll see if I can pick up a few extra shifts this week. 12 days is plenty of time to come up with the money."

Sam looks like he's about to argue, but his dad doesn't let him get a word in, giving his shoulder a squeeze and sildling back into the hallway.

"Come on, grab your coat! You'll miss the bus!"

"Coming," Sam mutters, turning away from the window and looking in on Jackie. She's so full of nerves that her egg tastes like rubber. She's pretending to enjoy it.

"Have a good day, Jackie," he whispers, giving her a little wave.

Jackie is so distracted that she waves back. She mentally kicks herself for the action; it wasn't prompted.

"Weird." Sam's eyebrows knit together in confusion. "It's like you understand me sometimes."

It takes all of her self-control to continue eating as normal. She'd love to talk to him, to let him know she hears everything he says, but that's the golden rule of FNL: residents cannot act outside of their predetermined course while the player is present. If they do, they risk the players reporting glitches and getting the server wiped. Jackie waits for the *click* of Sam's door before running back upstairs to her closet. She pulls on jeans and smoothes her dirty blonde hair into a ponytail. She has to find Marvin.

TWELVE DAYS

Marvin's player, Jamar, was the first of Sam's friends to switch to FNL 2.0. Marvin has been a little off ever since.

Jackie crosses her lawn into Marvin's, dodging a large collection of decorative garden gnomes and random pieces of metal. Jamar bought the gnomes, but the scaps are Marvin's doing. He's developed a fascination with pushing the boundaries of the game, becoming a bit of a tinkerer. He likes to find out what he can create himself with no player around to make purchases.

Jackie raises her fist to knock, but the door swings open before she even makes contact. "Saw you coming," Marvin says, gesturing to an old TV screen in the hall, multicolored wires sticking out of the back. Jackie peers at the screen, a blurry live feed of the gnomes making her smile.

"You got it working?" Jackie eyes the wires curiously, reaching out a hand to touch one.

Marvin's boney fingers slap hers away. "Don't!" He scolds. "That one is live." He turns away, already walking towards the kitchen. "Latte?"

"I'd love one," Jackie grins, following the swing of his braids around the corner. "What's new?" Marvin asks, clicking the portafilter out of his espresso machine.

Jackie slides onto a barstool, leaning her elbows on the counter. "A lot, actually. That's why I'm here."

"Oh? Can't just check in on your poor, lonely best friend?"

Jackie laughs. "Not this time." Her face falls. "I just heard Sam's dad say he wants to buy him 2.0 for Christmas."

Marvin drops a mug, the clay shattering on the tile floor. "What?

But—he can't afford that."

The remains of the mug blink in and out of existence before reappearing on the counter, fully mended.

"That's what Sam said," Jackie nods, "but his dad says he's going to pick up some extra shifts to make it happen."

Jackie's coffee drips into the drain, forgotten. "This is it, then," Marvin prophetizes. "He leaves, and we're done."

"We don't know that, Marv," Jackie tries to reassure him. "My interface could just go dark, and we could carry on as usual."

"That's the best case scenario. Even *if* that's all that happens, what's the *point*?" Marvin whines, sinking dramatically onto a barstool. "No players, nothing new to work with, just the same twelve neighbors surrounded by the same old stuff."

Jackie takes his hands in hers and says, "We'd all still have each other."

"You're so cheesy, Jacks," Marvin rolls his eyes, giving her a sad smile. "This is a real threat. I'm taking desolation, Jacquelyn. Like, everything dissolving into pixels, 0s and 1s instead of animation, darkness . . . we could just blink out of existence."

"We don't know that!" She repeats. "I haven't lost hope. There must be something we can do to convince Sam to keep playing."

"What, like, make the game more fun? Everyone knows you're already the perfect neighbor, what else could you do?"

"No, I mean I want to *tell* Sam! There has to be a way to show him we're really in here."

"Do you know how many times I tried to talk to Jamar? Jacks, you know the software garbles everything we say. You'd be wasting your breath."

Marvin stalks through the archway to the living room, flopping on the couch. Jackie follows, facing him with her hands on her hips. "I could glitch."

Marvin gapes up at her. "You wouldn't. He'll report you. Or want 2.0 even more."

"He won't," Jackie insists. "I know him, he cares about me. I glitched just this morning and waved at him by accident. He seemed suspicious, but only concerned."

"So you're just going to *wave* at him until he realizes you're alive?" Marvin's tone drips with sarcasm. "Good luck."

"Thank you," Jackie sniffs, ignoring his tone. "I'll need it. For all of us." She turns on her heel and marches out, determined to prove Marvin wrong.

ELEVEN DAYS

Jackie throws open the door to Marvin's house, storming through the kitchen and out the back door towards his shed-turned-workshop.

"He's an idiot! He's an unobservant nincompoop who refuses to acknowledge evidence that couldn't be more *clear*—"

"I'm guessing the waving didn't work," Marvin looks up from his workbench, round glasses perched on the end of his nose.

Jackie snorts. "No. I waved, I danced, I jumped up and down . . . nothing. He thought I was excited about the new porch chairs he bought last night."

"Are you?"

"Well, yes, but that's beside the point!"

Marvin smirks over his circuit board.

"Okay, Marv, you can be part of the problem or you can be part of the solution. If my idea was so stupid, let's hear a better one."

Marvin grabs a pair of pliers, not looking at her.

"Alright, yeah. You could try a physical distress signal. Bring furniture out onto the lawn and spell something out."

"Why does it sound like you don't think that will work?" Jackie says, frustrated with Marvin's apparent apathy.

"Because I don't. The software is just as likely to scramble a written word as it is anything we say. But until I get this up and running, it doesn't hurt to try."

Jackie leans across the counter.

"What are you making?"

"Not telling. Ask again tomorrow."

A little hurt by his bluntness, but used to his moods, she shrugs and wanders out, abandoning the sidewalk and strolling home directly through the gnomes.

TEN DAYS

"You were right," Jackie announces, heading straight for Marvin's drip coffee machine, the pot programmed to always be full. She doesn't have the patience for a latte this morning.

"I dragged the couch, side tables, and a bunch of other junk out onto the lawn. I even checked the view from the second floor, it clearly said 'HELLO.' But Sam just laughed and thought I wanted the couch on the porch. He kept it there and put the new porch chairs in the living room."

Jackie sinks onto the barstool beside Marvin, moving a thick reference book aside to make room for her mug. "It's a disaster."

Marvin hums, eyes rapidly scanning the pages of another textbook. "Sounds like it."

"What's all this?"

"Research."

"What for?"

"Still not telling. Hey, I need an antenna. Do you think you could get Sam to buy you a radio tonight?"

Jackie frowns. "Probably." She sips her coffee, an idea forming. "You'll have to come over, though. Dressed for a dance party."

"Not gonna happen."

NINE DAYS

"*Boogie Wonderland,*" Jackie sings, bursting through Marvin's back door.

He's on the couch in his pajamas, the old TV from the hallway now in pieces across the cushions, accompanied by what appears to be bits of her old karaoke machine.

Jackie holds out her shiny new boom box with pride.

"Easy," she grins. "The girls all came over, dressed to the nines. Wren even brought over a disco ball. We just stood around looking pathetic until Sam bought the radio."

Marvin's eyes light up as he extends the antenna.

"This is perfect. Thanks, Jacks."

"No problem," she yawns. "Coffee?"

"In the pot," he says distractedly, pulling out a screwdriver to dismantle his new toy.

Jackie crosses to the kitchen and helps herself, wandering back to watch Marvin sort the radio parts into the piles on the couch.

He stills, looking up at her, and takes a deep breath. "Jacquelyn, I think it's time to tell everyone. I don't think it's fair to keep this to ourselves."

Jackie had been thinking that, too. Just the thought of getting everyone together to explain makes her stomach tie itself in knots. She grips her coffee mug a little closer.

"Yeah . . . yeah, okay. I'll call a neighborhood meeting for tonight."

"I have to keep working," Marvin says, already securing the antenna onto the tip of a fishing pole.

Jackie sighs. "It's alright, I can handle them. I'm still waiting to hear what you're working *on*, though."

"Tomorrow."

EIGHT DAYS

Jackie finds Marvin in his back lawn, where there's even more scrap metal than gnomes. A wheelbarrow is propped up on cinder blocks. He's lying on his back underneath it, the way Frank down the street works on his cars.

"They didn't take it very well, Marv. You know how Wren gets under pressure. And Frank always argues about everything, even if you're just the messenger."

"Drill," Marvin orders, holding out his hand. Jackie places the drill in his palm.

"Since I told them, it's your turn to tell *me* what it is you're working on."

Marvin's open palm reappears. "Thicker drill bit."

"I'm serious," Jackie persists, digging through the tool box to find the part. "I don't see how poking holes in the bottom of a wheelbarrow is supposed to help me convince Sam we're all actually in here."

Marvin doesn't speak for a moment as the whirr of the drill fills the air. Finally, he wiggles out and sits up, sawdust stuck in his eyebrows.

"The holes are for securing the thing."

"And what's the thing?"

"I'm afraid to jinx it."

"Marvin!"

"Give me a few more days. You'll have to actually be on duty this weekend anyway. If I have any hope by Monday, I'll fill you in."

Jackie throws her hands up. "And what am I supposed to do until then? Just hang out with him as usual, pretending everything's fine?"

"Try to think of more ways to catch his attention. Brainstorm. He talks to you, listen to him."

FIVE DAYS

Marvin hands Jackie a steaming latte as he settles on her couch, still placed under the awning on her porch. Overnight, the software finally switched to Winter Mode, covering the grass beyond with a fresh blanket of snow. It matches the view out of Sam's bedroom window.

"So, I listened all weekend, just like you said, and I have a plan: we're gonna do a sit-in."

"What, like a protest?" Marvin adjusts his scarf.

"Yeah. Sam was working on his social studies homework and talking through it, as usual. His class is learning about nonviolent protests. That's what we have to do! Protest against him getting 2.0!"

"That'll get his attention, for sure. We've never tried to gather *everybody* in front of one interface while a player was watching." Marvin considers the idea. "He might think you're trying to have a party though, like when you had the girls over the other night."

"Oh, I didn't think of that," Jackie deflates a little.

Marvin gives her shoulder a nudge. "Hey, I still think it's a good idea. You should give it a shot tonight."

"You won't come?"

"I want to keep working. That's why I came over, I'm looking for any batteries you can spare."

"What, you can't just check in on your poor, lonely best friend?" Jackie throws his words back at him, nudging his leg with her foot. "You promised you'd tell!"

Marvin sighs, pulling his legs up and resting his chin on his knees. "Alright, yeah. Yeah, I mean, it's a little out there—"

"It's you, everything is," Jackie interrupts, laughing.

Marvin grins sheepishly. "Well, even for me."

He pauses. Jackie holds her breath.

"What if I told you I could make a translator?"

FOUR DAYS

"It had better fricken' work," Jackie pouts, dropping down onto a wicker porch chair beside her fireplace. She winces, both at how uncomfortable the chair is, and at the fact that it's in her living room in the first place.

"Language," Marvin says absently, pulling batteries out of a tacky dancing snowman on the coffee table.

Jackie huffs. "The sit-in was a total flop. You were right. Even though no one dressed up and we all just sat around not moving, he thought I was trying to throw Christmas party. *And* he thought the house itself was glitching because you took all the batteries yesterday."

"Hey, still a means to an end." He wiggles the snowman. "I was missing a few double AAs."

Jackie glares around her living room, now decked with strings of colorful lights and cheap Christmas decorations. "It's so ... loud."

"He went for quantity over quality this year, huh?" Marvin stands, looking around for his coat.

Jackie joins him. "I'll walk you home. I can't sit in here anymore."

"Fair enough."

Jackie gives the couch a forlorn glance as they cross her porch, leaving footprints in the snow across her yard. The snow makes the gnomes in Marvin's yard look like they're wearing little white caps.

Jackie smiles at the gnomes, then sighs. "How much longer do you think it'll take? I'm getting nervous, Marv. I feel like I'm not doing enough."

Marvin takes her arm as they cross onto his property. "Come on, you've had plenty of new ideas. Is there anything you want to try tonight?"

Jackie takes in a breath to respond, but trips, finding herself on the ground with a mouthful of snow.

Marvin cackles. "S- sorry, Jacks," he chokes out, pulling her up.

"Gosh dang gnomes!" Jackie squawks, wiping snow off her face and coat. She freezes, an idea igniting a light in her eyes. "Wait ... there *is* something we haven't tried."

THREE DAYS

"It was perfect! He was totally weirded out. Jamar is coming over tomorrow to see it for himself."

Marvin's head snaps up at the mention of his former player. "Wait, for real?"

"Yeah!" Jackie squeals and does a little dance, knocking over a box

68

of screws in Marvin's workshop. "Oops, sorry," she bends to gather the loose screws.

Marvin sets his glasses on the counter and leans back, cracking his knuckles. "I guess that did the trick. The game certainly isn't supposed to randomly populate 76 gnomes onto a perfectly nice lawn."

Jackie giggles, presenting Marvin with the now tidy box of screws.

He snatches it back. "Thanks, I actually do need these next. And— can you go grab the wheelbarrow and get the snow off of it?"

Jackie nods. "Do you think we can finish this before tomorrow?"

"We have to try."

TWO DAYS

"Merry Christmas Eve!" Sam grins in at Jackie, who jumps out of bed as usual. She yawns and waves, then makes her bed as Sam checks her bank statement.

"Do you want me to get you a tree? I'm cutting down a tree with Dad today, we can match!"

Jackie does a little dance to show yes, she would like a Christmas tree.

"Hang on," Sam says, his eyes losing focus. He's scrolling through the holiday catalog, a pop-up on his screen.

Jackie hurries downstairs, sure he's about to put it in the living room. While the rest of the decorations might not be to her taste, how badly can you mess up a Christmas tree?

"Yes, there! Now THAT's a tree!"

Jackie resists the urge to roll her eyes. Sam had chosen an evergreen with an astronaut theme. It matches absolutely nothing in the room, but at least the star on top is impressive.

"Ready to hit the road?" Dad calls from out of sight.

"Just a sec!" Sam replies, pulling on his mittens.

To Jackie, he says, "Don't forget Jamar's coming over later. He wants to try and figure out how the gnomes got in your yard."

Jackie sighs and grabs a muffin from the kitchen, alternating between taking bites and getting dressed for the walk to Marvin's house. She pauses on the porch, admiring the view of all 76 stolen gnomes.

Jackie finds herself smiling, despite everything. It had been an out-of-the-box idea, but she'd finally shown Sam there was more to this game than he realized. *She* was more than he realized.

Her gaze drifts up to the interface. She can see a glimmer of Christmas lights on the oak tree through Sam's bedroom window. Snow is drifting down in steady flakes, both in the outside world and in the game. She puts her head down and crosses her lawn, careful not to trip on the gnomes.

Marvin is in his workshop, right where she expected him to be.

"Good morning!" she chirps, knocking the snow from her boots.

Without looking up, he points at a thermos balanced on a stack of cardboard boxes.

Jackie grins and takes a sip, the latte warming her from the inside. She's content to watch Marvin work, admiring his dedication and persistence.

After a moment, he sits back on his heels from his spot near the floor, adjusting the tethers on the wheelbarrow. "Alright, that's about all I can do. Either it works or it doesn't."

"Only one way to find out!" Jackie tucks the thermos in her pocket. "Let's wheel it over to my place."

Sam is only gone for a few hours, but it feels like a lifetime. Jackie and Marvin park the wheelbarrow in front of the porch, then sit on the couch and attempt to enjoy their coffee while watching the Christmas lights in Sam's world flicker. As Jackie's nerves build, her coffee starts tasting more and more like acid.

"What if he doesn't like me?"

"Jacks, he talks to you more than he talks to his own father."

"What if he still wants to get 2.0?"

"He didn't even want to in the first place, I'm sure you can convince him to keep playing."

"What if . . ."

Marvin patiently fields each new worry with a reasonable response. With his project complete, he's much more calm than before.

"How are you not freaking out?" Jackie finally asks. She's taken to pacing the length of the porch.

"It's a matter of practicality, Jacks. If it works, that's great, if it doesn't . . . There's nothing we can do about that now. We can go into the void knowing we gave it our all."

"What about Jamar?"

"What about him?" Marvin tenses, crossing his arms. "He gave up on me a long time ago." He doesn't meet Jackie's eyes.

"That doesn't mean you have to pretend not to miss him," Jackie says, settling beside him on the couch. "This is a chance to talk to him, to tell him how you feel. Have you decided what to say?"

They hear Sam's front door bang open, several pairs of boots stomping around.

Marvin swallows, gloved fingers laced tight together. "I'm not saying anything. This is about you and Sam and getting Sam to stay. Jamar doesn't have to—"

"Bro!" comes a shout from the hallway.

Marvin freezes. Jackie smiles, squeezing his hand.

"Dude, maybe help?" They hear Sam respond, laughing. "Man, it's a big tree!"

There's more rustling. Something goes *thud*.

"Careful of the floor, boys, no scratching!" Dad calls.

Inside the game, Jackie and Marvin freeze, listening to the kids bicker over how to balance the tree and secure it in its stand.

Finally, Sam comes into view, taking off his beanie.

"It goes like, *whoop,*" Sam barks a laugh, using his neck to imitate the tree scrunched up against the ceiling.

Jamar drops his backpack, grinning. "That's your biggest one yet!" He catches sight of the screen. "You got FNL up already?"

"Yeah, all day! Pull up that chair," Sam points to his half-dirty laundry chair and settles in at his desk. "Hey, what's this wheelbarrow of junk?"

Jamar dumps the clothes on the ground and swings the chair around to join Sam. "Bro, what? How is Marvin there?"

"Whadaya mean? He's over all the time. Most of the neighbors were over the other night, they're always doing that."

Jackie steels herself and stands up, making her way to the wheelbarrow.

"The game isn't programmed to let the neighbors just hang out like that, without us playing. They should have gone dormant by now, deactivated." Jamar takes up the whole interface as he squints in at them. "And yeah, how the heck did all my gnomes make it over here? I'm grabbing my laptop. I wanna see if I can log back into the old version."

Marvin leaps to his feet. "Wait, no!" he shouts, sprinting back across the lawn towards his workshop.

"Marvin!" Jackie calls, running after him. She makes it to the line between their properties but slams against the invisible wall, cursing. Free Roam deactivates when the player is online.

"Dude, they're being really weird . . ." Sam says over his shoulder. Jackie spins to face him, glimpsing Jamar on his laptop in the background.

"I'm in!" Jamar says, holding his laptop on his knee. "Holy shh . . ."

Jackie turns back around just in time to see Marvin's interface blink to life for the first time in almost a year. Marvin's house blocks most of her view, but there's Jamar, staring out at the wreckage of what he once designed.

"Man, there's junk *everywhere!*" Sam leans over Jamar's shoulder.

Jamar scrolls around, taking in the scraps and half-finished gadgets littering the house and buried under the snow on the lawn. "And all my gnomes are gone!"

Jumping between the gnomes, Jackie hurries back to the translator.

Remembering the sequence Marvin taught her, she tugs on the pull cord from Frank's old lawnmower, flicks on the switches from Wren's basement lights, and pushes the ON button connected to the batteries from her dancing snowman.

She doesn't breathe.

To Jackie's relief, the contraption sputters to life, blinking and whirring in several different places. Ignoring Sam's dumbfounded look, she unhooks her old karaoke microphone and takes a deep breath.

"Sam?" she asks. Her voice echoes around her, louder than usual, with a tinny quality. Both boys freeze, staring in at her. Jamar looks like he's about to faint.

Jackie grins, heart pounding. "You can understand me?"

Sam blinks, then nods, too stunned to speak.

"Good. I have a lot to explain."

CHRISTMAS

"Ho, ho, ho!" Sam's dad bursts into his room. He's dressed head to toe in Santa gear, a brown sack slung over his shoulder.

Sam yelps, startling awake. "Daaaad! You gotta stop doing that, I'm too old!"

"No one's too old for Santa! Hey, bet you won't be complaining about what Santa brought you this year . . ." He reaches into his sack and pulls out a decorative card.

Jackie gives up pretending to sleep and sits on the edge of her bed, watching.

Sam rubs his eyes and smiles at his dad's antics, despite himself. He opens the card and grins. "A PlayStart gift card!"

"I went in there but I didn't wanna pull a Classic Dad and buy the wrong game . . . so, I thought we could go together tomorrow and you can pick it out yourself." He ruffles Sam's hair. "How does that sound?"

Sam fixes his hair and glances over at Jackie, who gives him a big grin and a wave.

"Actually . . . I think I wanna buy a couple expansion packs for the one I already have. When Jamar was over yesterday, he pulled up the old version, and we were talking about having Thalia and Riley hop back on, too. Get the neighborhood back together again."

"That sounds great, kiddo," Dad gives him a fond smile, backing out the door. "Alright, pancakes are in the kitchen when you're ready."

"Yep, just give me a sec," Sam stands and stretches, pulling on reindeer slippers. Jackie wraps a snowman robe around herself and trots downstairs.

"Merry Christmas, Jackie," Sam's goofy grin comes into view.

Jackie picks up her mic. "Merry Christmas, Sam!"

"Say Merry Christmas to Marvin for me? Here, I'll hit Free Roam."

She beams. "Will do, thanks. Enjoy the pancakes!"

A few minutes later, Jackie gapes at the pile of brand-new electronics under Marvin's last-minute tree.

"He bought me one of each kitchen appliance! And two laptops! And a HUGE toolbox!" Marvin claps, rubbing his hands together.

"Betcha he bought coins with *real* money last night," Jackie laughs. "You certainly haven't 'worked' in months!"

Marvin laughs. "Well, I love them, but he's out of luck if he thinks he can buy my forgiveness. He'll be in the doghouse for a while."

Jackie smiles and shakes her head, backing into the kitchen to fill a mug of drip coffee. "Go easy on him, Marv. There's no way he could have known."

"Humph," grunts Marvin, joining her at the breakfast bar.

They stare at his mountain of gifts, then at each other, grinning from ear to ear.

"Merry Christmas, Marv," Jackie knocks her knee against his. "And thank you."

"Of course," Marvin squeezes her arm. "Merry Christmas, Jacks."

What The Fae

by Isha Repal

"Not the car stealing one! It's so lame and after what Jake did to the police chief, Zabia needs her dare to up the ante!"

A girl with beautiful golden hair tied in a ponytail thumped her fist on the round table we all sat at. That's Cyndie, my best friend who usually has my wellbeing in her mind but not today. Today was the day we were all discussing my birthday dare. It was a tradition Cyndie's brother, Jake had started during his tenth party announcing it to be boring and needing a challenge that was worth his double-digit big day.

To discuss this *very important* tradition we sat in Madam Marie's Menu, a local deli with the best soups and sandwiches. Situated just near our small downtown it has been our hangout place for years. I looked at Jake wondering how to bring up my idea, although Jake was huge and burly took things as they were, thus the best target.

Jake was blond like Cyndie and the more outspoken of the three siblings. Yes, three. Jake had a fraternal twin and the only dark-haired Rhoda kid, Samir. He was obviously the shiniest (with a tongue *and* a nose piercing, not counting all the ear studs, you are shiny!) and smartest of the three. And he was scrutinizing his cup of coffee ignoring the back and forth of his siblings. *What was so important in that cup?*

Jake clicked his tongue, "Not my fault, the officers got used to our pattern! How about going to Mister William's farm and getting his dog?"

Cyndie crunched her face and shook her head. "No. That won't do. The dog likes her, it would be too easy." She then glared at me as if it was my fault!

I cleared my throat and suggested, "What about the fae tree?"

That got everyone's attention, and Samir looked up from his coffee to raise an eyebrow at me. "The fae tree?"

Trying hard to ignore the cold sweat gathering on my palms I continued, "Yes, you know from the tale. The tree with the human face that is in the center of the forest. I can livestream it on the group for you all." *Please take the bait. I need to follow the journal!*

Jake snorted, "You know your way in and out of that forest better than anyone here, not a chance." His hands moved with his words and swung down at the rejection, another difference with Samir who sat still as a statue.

"No wait." Cyndie sat up from her seat and leaned forward. "How well do you know the place at *night*?"

There it was. I gulped the saliva pooled in my mouth and shakily said, "I haven't been there in the dark. Wasn't allowed by mother and followed her wishes after she . . . passed on."

There was a tense silence for some time before Cyndie broke it by giggling. "I bet five hundred quid that you run back with your ass hanging out."

"I say a thousand that she lasts for an hour but passes out. That's a lot of courage for *her*."

I love my friends, I really do. But it's times like this where you just must whack some sense in their heads with a cast iron skillet. I clicked my tongue in feigned annoyance, it's times like this I wished I had the power from the old tales to turn them into frogs and throw them in a river.

There was snickering all around the table we sat at for our weekend kiddie drinks. I could see Madam Marie's lips quiver slightly and never have I felt so offended! Even she thought the dare was beyond me.

I sniffed haughtily and turned up my chin, "Well, you'll all be eating your words soon. The full moon's in three days. The lore says that's the best time to hunt faeries."

Hearing this, even people at the tables around us laughed out loudly, not even ashamed to be caught eavesdropping on kids. A man with a bushy beard and warm eyes turned around and slapped the back of his chair.

"Zabia, kid, hunting fae is a myth. You have got more chances of hunting rabbits in the forest." He mocked, "Get some rabbit feet for me will ya? I put in five thousand. Enjoy!"

Our townsfolk were as weird as our folklore. They heartily believed and worshiped the power of fae. They believed in the stories of witches and the curses of fae but deemed them too untouchable by humans and concluded that *hunting* them was impossible.

I huffed, "Fine, Mr. Scam. Just you wait when I return richer than ever!"

Madam Marie thumped four beer glasses on our table and successfully silenced everyone. Our glasses contained apple juice as we weren't quite sixteen yet, unlike the adults who had already gotten drunk.

"Zabia! If you must continue this foolishness, take your alarm with you. You never know the danger in those woods."

Guilt washed over me as I looked into her concerned green eyes. Madam Marie practically raised me in her small tavern after my mother's death. I owe a lot to her, but this was one thing I couldn't step back from.

I faked a smile and whispered, "No worries, Marie. Nothing's gonna happen in there."

Cyndie snorted from beside me, using her fingers to twirl a circle in the air, "Madam, please. Like this little thing has the guts to stay after it gets dark in here."

Madam Marie smiled as she carried away the trash and left us alone. Even the old men started to turn away as they lost interest in the conversation.

I slapped Cyndie's hand away from where it was creeping up my face, "Stop that. And. I. AM. NOT. LITTLE! I'm almost sixteen! I have lots of growing left to do yet."

Instead of the sympathy I was expecting, all I felt was a lot of patting on my head, fluffing my already messy hair. Jake and Samir didn't help things by emphasizing their ridiculously tall bodies as they didn't bother leaning forward across the table to do so. Ever since they hit puberty and hit the growth spurts, they have taken every chance to tease my small height since *I was so cute!* I hope they feel the burning anger from all the short people living world wide and beg for forgiveness.

The world really wasn't fair.

Jake shrugged and went back to tracing the water droplets on his condensed beer glass. "She didn't get her parents' genes is all I am saying. Look at her father—"

"Jake," Cyndie interrupted, glaring at his now sheepish face. "We don't talk about that trash can."

Jake murmured an apology before changing the subject. "Anyways, Zabia, take your emergency phone with you. Stream your journey. We will be watching but won't be able to chat."

Samir, who had been silent till now, tapped his finger on the table. "So to summarize: Zabia, you will be going this full moon at midnight to search for The Tree. You will record your results and come back, right?" He looked up and my heart thumped at his glance.

Why again?! Stupid crushes on tall, dark haired wild boys. Shaking away distracting thoughts I nodded, "Yep. And a stalker alarm to soothe Madam Marie," I added.

Samir smiled his crooked smile that never once stopped making me warm inside. "Okay, let's all shake on it."

He put his hand palm down on the table, waiting for the others.

Jake over enthusiastically slapped his hand on his brother's. "Yeah! Let's do this, for Zabia's initiation and the five thousand quid on the line."

Samir glared at Jake's hand but let out a sigh. After all, nothing could change the bone headedness coursing through that idiot. Cyndie flipped her golden hair back as she finished her juice and slammed the empty glass down. "To Zabia's initiation, the only fifteen-year-old in the group. To our little charmer." She too slapped her hand on the stack and grinned wildly.

I swore back a retort. Only these shitty kids could act drunk without actually getting drunk.

Raising my hand, I slowly slipped it on Cyndie's, feeling bad for

Samir's lone hand enduring all those slaps. "To my initiation and to prove your trashy asses wrong!"

"YEAH!!!!!"

§

My name is Zabia Crow, and I live in the *lovely* town of the Fallen. Notice my pointed and heavy sarcasm.

Not to say that the Fallen is a bad place, but the folks in it killed my mother, how am I still supposed to like it? Not counting Madam Marie's restaurant or Angela's thrift store or the Emersons park by the cliff. There is unfinished business between the town elders and me, but the rest of the town, ignorant to that night, is chill. But I hold a deep grudge and would come back for them.

Let me start again from the beginning.

My name is Zabia Crow from the Fallen. Our folktales revolve around the fae. Yep, the little fairy-like creatures that make the town sound even more flashy and glittery (I mean who names a town The Fallen? A grade-schooler?).

But I digress.

Along with creatures of fae-world, the villagers are obsessed with people with the occult: aka witches. A hypocritical obsession, since they want the powers for themselves not the people.

My mother was *not* one of them. My mother belonged to one of the founding families of the Fallen, which died out when she married into my father's family. She was a healer and used the forest herbs and the knowledge of herbology to tend to the client's wounds and various illnesses.

I know she used science and not some fancy schmancy voodoo, I have read the books she painstakingly wrote after experimenting on herself. She also had a Master's degree in clinical sciences. Did that make the people see her differently? No.

The townsmen didn't like that my mother was an independent, young woman. The thought of *her* having a miniscule connection to the power of fae made them greedy and angry. Hence, she was tied to a stake in the town square and the men chosen by the elders stoned her to death at midnight on my seventh birthday.

After that my father seemingly started to like the company of alcohol more than me and at times, left the house to spend days at the back-alley taverns far away from the town square. During my visit to my mother's grave last year, I saw him sit in the back of a red van and leave with a small backpack. That was the last I saw him.

I fondly remember the days my mother would sit me down and teach me her practice. I used to have fun, and it also helped me understand the brews and medicinal concoctions. Along with all the cutting, slicing, grinding, and tempering of the various ingredients, she would encourage me to pray to a god, as if asking permission to use the ingredients. Mother used to say the fae were based on these gods, and my mind would wander the moment her lectures ventured into the *philosophical* part of the process.

She would light candles and let the fresh vanilla scent waft over the house.

"Zabia, you should always focus on an entity when working with nature. You don't want to anger any spirits. Entities help you in cultivating your energy." She used to say as she poured the ground compounds from the mortar into a small bowl and caress it slightly, her old family signet clanking on the porcelain. She would then close her eyes and pray. Apparently, this was as age-old method from her maternal family, whose coat of arms she always wore.

Later she would spoon in honey or whatever was required on a particular recipe, and mix it. The colors in the bowl would always change, not one like the other. She wholeheartedly believed in the town folklore and myths of the fae-world—believed that there were fae around us who were not bad, that there would be fae who would one day connect with us spiritually.

"Zabia, the fae live in a world like ours. They are good beings. Don't hunt them!"

Ironic, considering her fellow believers of fae killed her rather than the maniacal faeries. The village elders took great care in their words surrounding fae and they always considered the myths to be powerful but filled with negativity. After mother's death, I grew up with those words.

The eight long, hard years without her were made a bit better with the introduction of Cyndie and her brothers; Jake and Samir. A small family of five with two indulging parents who raised three rascals with loads of love. They didn't mind cherishing a fourth child, much to my then childish surprise.

The Rhoda family moved to the Fallen during my early teenage years and helped me from getting too deep in my head. They were the family I needed after my parents left me alone, other than Madam Marie of course.

But I still couldn't let go of my mom's death and the conspiracy surrounding it. The feeling grew with time and peaked last month, when I cleaned out my parents' room. I always had a hard time going through mother's stuff and after father left last year, I locked the room. Alas, it was time for deep cleaning and I couldn't let the house rest in dust.

I started with vacuuming and moved on to dusting when I found a super-secret journal hidden in their closet. My finger caught on to a wooden edge sticking out and accidentally pulled it up, leading to a lever slowly opening a compartment camouflaged with the back of the closet. I was dumbfounded that mother did this and wondered if this was the reason why she died?

It was an old leather-bound book, palm-sized and with its pages beginning to yellow and curl on the edges.

I had opened it then in curiosity which grew even more after I saw what was stuffed inside.

There nestled among the empty yellow pages was a map. I had flipped through them to see if anything was written, but it was as empty as it was upon my first glance.

The map though was not just any map, I recognized it as a map of the forest where my mother and I used to forage for herbs. It was an ordinary map if not for the suspicious X sketched in charcoal, marked over a grove of trees in the middle of the forest, a full moon drawn beside it.

It was a happy coincidence that the Rhoda kids and I had the long-standing tradition of celebrating birthdays in a grand way. I tried not to regret manipulating them into challenging me to go into the forest in the dark, but my mother's matters seemed to weigh more on my emotional scale.

I shook out of my reverie as Jake's hand thumped loudly against my back. I looked up and saw Samir looking at me in concern which I good-heartedly waved off. I muttered a good bye, pointedly ignoring Cyndie's wink as she walked in the house after her brothers and waited till they all were removed from my sight. Heaving a sigh, I took out a crumpled piece of paper and looked down at the map, there was so much work to do.

§

Three days later I stepped into the haunting line of the trees that loomed over me. I didn't want to agree with Cyndie, but yes, I was a proud coward in my heart. The dark scared me like no other, unless there was a distraction.

It was late at night and the forests looked menacing. My hands shook, making my flashlight beam bounce every now and then. I had been scoping this place that morning to map out the way and the tree; however, the silence made it ten times creepier. Gulping down my fear, I flashed the light on the nearby tree trunks looking for my marks. Neon ribbons knotted with a birch branch, not so easy to look for at night with scarce moonlight filtering through the dense branches.

Damn those pigs! Thinking of my traitorous friends made me sick to my stomach, as I recalled them waving me off with hands full of popcorn and pointing to the phone as a reminder.

Speaking of . . . I shuffled my stuff in one hand and grasped out a water bottle from the rucksack over my back. Obviously, it didn't have any H_2O but caffeine mixed with soda to soothe my nerves.

I emptied the bottle in a few minutes and gave out a sigh of relief. Now the forest didn't seem so scary, which was the point. Now to start the damn stream. The cold made it harder but I got the livestream started. I squinted at the screen and saw three views.

At least, the traitors were awake with me.

Snorting, I flipped the camera to the face at the trees. Legs stumbling through the tough and big tree roots I reached that one tree I had marked.

One of the myths in our town surrounded a particular tree with a black bark and roots, with drooping leaves and a human face carved on its trunk. With five-thousand quid on the line, I went through hell to look for the tree matching its description, which coincidentally matched the X on the map. *What was mom doing with this? And how come no one else has reached this point???*

Was the myth created to scare naughty children away from a random repulsive tree? I looked at the face on the tree through the phone camera and shivered in revulsion. It looked so real and alive, almost as if someone was sleeping *inside* the tree.

Stopping my movements for a second, I thought back to the myth, *the roots of the tree will have the portal to the faeland.* I immediately looked down and searched around for a door like a fool. I almost found nothing but a decayed black flag that stood out from the other wooden roots. That was new and suspicious.

Why was it even a myth? Why was my mom killed for believing in the myth our village created? Scoffing at the hypocrisy, I got down to digging.

After what felt like ten minutes, I set up my phone up on a tripod stand, focused it on the spot I was digging, and went back to the rucksack I had thrown aside, to remove a shovel. An hour later, I had almost given up when the shovel struck metal, a clang echoing through the otherwise silent forest.

My eyes got wide in surprise and I turned to the phone, "Do you hear that, guys?"

Euphoria spread through my chest, as a feeling of accomplishment filled me. *Was it treasure?!*

"I am shutting off the stream, it's been an hour. So, I have won the bet and the money." I gave a two-finger salute and packed the phone away and gave all my attention to the hole.

I hurriedly dug the metal thing out and it looked to be a chest, even better! Pulling it out, I set about cleaning it. I looked through my rucksack and opened a pure mineral water bottle and a washcloth, and thoroughly wiped the chest.

The cleaned chest was small with a lock on it. Peering at it closely, I changed my observation. An old, rusted lock. The shovel had a second use.

Hitting it a few times did the trick and the lock cracked open, falling onto the ground with soft thud, the dry and wet leaves crumpled with the unexpected weight. I could feel my heart thumping loudly as excitement and hesitance took over.

X marks the spot. What was my mom hiding after all this time?!

I slowly lifted the lid open, and my heart dropped. A cold wave hit my back and sweat dripped down my spine.

There were bones inside, *child-sized bones!*

A streak of moonlight fell in front of me and I turned the chest to look inside properly. Then the bones started shimmering and I saw a cloth lying underneath the bones. Creeped out, I put my hand in and shuffled through the bones and tried to pull the cloth out. If nothing else, the cloth would work as evidence for the dare and for me to look deeper tomorrow. In broad daylight.

My insides churned with restlessness and guilt as I looked down at the chest. I had a gut feeling that I shouldn't mix up the Rhodas in my mother's mystery yet, they were good people and didn't deserve to be used.

Except the cloth didn't feel like a cloth. It gave the same feeling my mother's diary gave, malleable leather but once alive.

Swallowing my saliva, I looked at the bones closely. Size of a child, with leather cloth attached to the body. I peered at the glittering cloth with squinted eyes and my mouth dropped open.

No, those were wings! Wings attached to the bones. My gaze moved up to the skull and wasn't surprised to see fangs creeping out of the mouth. They fit the image told by the myths.

Bloody hell, my mom was right! Fae exist in our world!

But then my blood ran cold. Because there, clutched in the fingers of the dead fairy, was a ring, a familiar ring I remember used to be worn by my mother when she was alive. The family coat of arms glinted in the meek light and twinkled.

How did it get here and when?

Horology.

by Hannah Penn

I was given a day.
And I watched
as the finite sand
edged through the cracks
and gathered,
tightly packed,
in a pile below.
I used to be infinite,
but the day was as finite
as the sight before me.
I crafted this measurement,
this system of time.
I was given a day.

I tended to life
as days past and gone.
Watched as the sand
poured through.
And I counted my breaths,
my blinks,
my sighs.
And stood watching
as infinite
became finite.

And I didn't wish,
didn't plead,
didn't cry.
Simply counted the makings
of time in a day.
I sat
and I pondered
and stared straight ahead,
until dusk turned to night,
and the pile tumbled over.

I was given a day,
and what a day was had.
I sat back in my chair
and stopped counting
my breaths,
my blinks,
my sighs.
I sat watching as the sand
blew away,
and infinity
was restored once again.

Anomal Amalgam

by Shea Dunlop

The snowdrift twitched. Kiri kept perfectly still, from the tip of her mottled snout to the end of her barbed tail. She could tell the vole wasn't large, but it was something. A snack to keep her stomach from rumbling and alerting the larger game.

Cautiously, she inched a forepaw ahead. Then another. She opened her jaws ever so slowly, ready to scoop up both the vole and the snow on top of it. Her nostrils flared as she inhaled, and—

Sneezed.

With a tiny squeak, the vole shot out from its chilly oasis and darted across the expanse of icy crust between Kiri and the edge of the clearing. She briefly considered giving chase, but rejected the idea with a dismissive flick of her wing. Not worth the energy for such a measly morsel. Snaking back up her favorite stakeout tree, her scales blending into the leafless bark, Kiri resolved to wait for something more worth her while. A pair of rabbits, perhaps. Or maybe even a wild goat!

That was quite the thought. Bored, she began to daydream about the look on her cave mate's face should she manage to bring home such a large prize. She'd struggle to pull the animal over the pass, it being slightly larger than her, but if she could just get to the entrance of the System, the guards might be convinced to help her carry the goat to the second level. There, Nonna would be waiting with her floured apron on and gray hair all in a frizz. It would make her year. Kiri hated seeing Nonna so skinny.

The other dragons had thought her quite odd for pairing with Nonna. On Bonding Day, most fledgling dragons competed to pick the best young hunter, fighter, or blacksmith from among the unBonded humans in the System. Someone with whom they could build a life and make a living.

Never one for confrontation, and lacking an affinity for any particular skills, Kiri hadn't exactly had first pick of the unBonded humans.

In fact, she'd been dead last.

Clambering up onto the dais, Kiri had gazed down into a sea of hopeful faces. Young men hoping to impress their amour by winning the attention of a dragon. Mothers with mouths to feed, desperate for a stroke of luck. Humans of every sort, wanting something from her. Some form of glory she wasn't at all confident she'd be able to deliver.

And then there was Nonna, known as Cardea at the time. The spinster, odd strands of silver shooting through her tangled dark hair, was standing near the back appearing almost apologetic. While the System Leaders mandated that every human present themselves to the dragons each year for Bonding, it wasn't a punishment; most would gladly chop off an arm for the opportunity. But the willowy Cardea had just offered Kiri a small smile of understanding.

It's alright, she seemed to say, *you needn't consider me. I know I'm nobody's first choice.*

Spreading her wings and launching into the air, Kiri had circled over the crowd twice, only to drift down and land gently upon the spinster's shoulder. She'd ridden back to Cardea's cave with the outraged murmurs of the crowd echoing behind her and the certainty she'd chosen her perfect match.

Kiri let out a huff of amusement, remembering the days when she could ride around on Nonna's shoulder. If she tried that now, the aging woman would collapse, though Kiri was admittedly not very heavy by the standards of her kind.

In contrast, Kiri spotted Uto soaring above her, his bulky bronze form casting a direct shadow in the midday sun. The guard dragon was an unusually large specimen, one of the few just the right size to carry one small human. Luckily, Buxton wasn't a large man. Kiri could make out Uto's companion riding between his wings, dressed for battle.

From her vantage point high in the trees, Kiri could feel Uto emitting **triumph** and **satisfaction**. She guessed he was heading back from attacking the bandit wagon train a scout dragon had reported last night beyond the rise of the mountain east of this clearing. The noise from the skirmish had disturbed her hunting this morning, but no matter. Better to take them out now than let them get close to the System.

Although she doubted Uto or Buxton cared what she thought, she sent **gratitude** in their direction anyway. Theirs was a tough job she wouldn't care to perform herself.

She'd never formally picked up a trade or joined the workforce like so many of her brethren. She was content to hunt to feed herself and Nonna. They traded what they could for grapes and other fruits, Nonna turning a bit of a profit off of her knack for winemaking.

On the whole, Kiri felt too anomic to be of use to the System. She was never antagonized but never included. She couldn't bring herself to hold the same values and ideals as the other dragons and their companions, those that praised the System and did everything in their power to contribute to its wealth. Kiri just did what was required to live a simple life. And if it made her and Nonna outcasts, so be it. She was happy just the way they were, thank you very much.

Lost in her thoughts, the day slipped by with little excitement. Kiri even caught herself dozing in her tree as the sun began to slip behind the snow-covered slope of the valley. Shaking herself, she stretched languidly on her branch, disturbing the winter finches in a neighboring tree. Better to head home early and avoid the sunless chill already creeping through the edges of the forest.

Lightly hopping to the frozen ground, Kiri tensed her hind legs, preparing to take off. She hesitated, catching a slight hissing noise coming from the East. She cocked her head, listening. It didn't sound like any prey that should be out in the wintertime. If anything, she would have guessed it was a snake slithering through the underbrush, but there was nothing to slither through other than piles of snow.

It was getting louder.

Cautious, Kiri backed away and wriggled under a frosted shrub, unsure whether to flee or simply hide. The hissing increased, accompanied by the crunch of twigs breaking, and . . . laughter?

Kiri tensed, unsure if this human would be a friend or a foe.

The snowbank where Kiri had lost the vole exploded in a shower of icy chunks. She briefly closed her eyes against the onslaught but hurriedly blinked away the moisture, eager to spot the source of the commotion.

In the center of the clearing sat a human child on a splintered board of oak. He was giggling, exhilarated from his slide down the hill, until he abruptly stopped with a loud hiccup. He began to wail.

Kiri remained motionless beneath the shrub, staring at the interloper. She had no experience with the hatchlings of humans and did not particularly want to involve herself with this one. However, the child was obviously distressed, and Kiri didn't feel right just slipping away without investigating further.

She poked her snout out from under the branches, scenting the air with her tongue for increased accuracy. The sting of smoke was unmistakable around the boy, clinging to his winter furs like a bothersome burr.

After a few more moments of deliberation, Kiri shouldered through the edge of the shrub and slowly approached the boy. She made it halfway toward him before his tears forced him to take a breath, eyes widening at the sight of her. She ceased her advance, close enough to notice the glow of his golden skin against the snow, but far enough back not to scare him too much, she hoped.

He gazed at her, mouth frozen in a surprised "O," misery momentarily forgotten.

Though she knew it wouldn't mean anything to him, she couldn't stop herself from radiating **concern**.

He blinked, and sent **confusion** right back.

Kiri stared. In the stillness of the moment, the pounding of her heart seemed louder than festival drums.

Never in her three decades of life had a human sent her an emotion. She didn't even think it was possible for them to do. Kiri understood humans had much the same emotional range as dragons, of course, but they had to use spoken language to communicate those feelings. Yet here was this lost little boy, emoting. Unmistakably communicating in her native language.

Kiri responded with **shock** before she even realized she was emoting. She quickly mastered herself and followed up with **concern** again, sending **curiosity** for good measure. She was hoping the child could give her some indication of how and why he had come to be here, alone, in the middle of winter.

He wrinkled his nose at her, appearing unsure of whether or not to offer his trust.

Although no taller than the boy, it occurred to Kiri that her stance might indicate an attempt at dominance over him. She held his gaze and crouched flat in the snow, allowing him the higher ground.

This seemed to work; Kiri watched some of the tension in his slight shoulders melt away.

He blinked a few more times, then indicated he was unharmed by holding up his arms and shaking his legs out in front of him. She already didn't know what to do with a stranded toddler, much less an injured one, so she was pleased to confirm he hadn't broken any bones.

In that strange, mature manner of his, he returned his gaze to hers and sent her **surprise, anxiety, fear,** and **determination** all in quick succession. He pointed up at the sky and then to her. Making an explosion gesture with his gloved hands, he added a "BOOOM!" sound effect, pushing air through his lips. He giggled. Then quietly began to cry again.

Kiri couldn't believe she was communicating with a human as naturally as she would with a littermate. He understood just how to string together his emotions to tell his story. He even had the advantage of human gesture to aid his feelings!

Based on his energetic reenactment, she gathered that he must have been part of the wagon train Uto attacked this morning. It was surprising Uto had left any survivors at all, but perhaps the child (or his parents) had managed to smuggle him away in the confusion.

Kiri wasn't sure if he was old enough to use his words, she knew human children didn't quite master that for some years. She couldn't help but think that once he did, he could play a key role in communication between dragons and humans.

Though human language was easy to comprehend, dragons didn't have the proper anatomy to respond in kind. Then there was the fact that only the humans Bonded with a dragon could interpret a dragon's emotions. Aside from this little one, Kiri had never heard tell of human who could emote in return. They typically used their own language to respond. While it was impossible for a dragon to send an emotion they weren't feeling, humans could say one thing and mean another. This made them untrustworthy, and dragons susceptible to trickery.

A human who could emote would not be able to lie to a dragon. This boy could be a true ambassador, able to judge fairly. He could be powerful enough to rule the System if he wished. Such a man would oust the Leaders in a vote, no matter how rigged; the dragons would stand for no one else to unify the two species once and for all.

Kiri was reluctant to take responsibility for the child, but she could see no other option unless she were to strand him in the forest. Had he been simply the child of an enemy, she might have considered it, but his abilities made him too significant to abandon.

Continuing her slow approach towards him, she radiated **calm** and **comfort**, doing what she could to ease his unrest. Somehow, Kiri had to convince him to trust her enough to climb on her back. She was much too small for an adult to mount, but she thought she could handle a human this light and didn't see any other way to get him over the pass to the entrance of the System.

In her growing proximity, he appeared to forget his woes. He obviously hadn't seen many dragons, perhaps none, before Uto this morning. He stretched out a mitt towards her.

Kiri allowed him to touch her brow.

His round face split into a cherubic grin as he giggled again. Relieved, Kiri aligned herself next to him, facing the same direction as his makeshift sled. She turned her neck and gestured with her snout, emitting **anticipation**.

Miraculously, he understood. Still giggling, he clambered off his sled and gripped one of the blunt spikes along her spine, pulling himself up over a wing. Kiri hoped he had the sense to hold on.

Using the sled as a launchpad, Kiri crouched and sprung upward, forcing her wings to push the air below her even with the added weight on her back. The child let out a yelp of alarm, but his grip was firm, and Kiri ceased worrying about his safety as she continued to climb. The flight was short, and even if he fell, she felt confident she could catch him in time.

As she flew, the boy emoted constantly: **elation, fear,** and **wonder** being natural responses to a first flight. Kiri felt a glow in her chest, anticipating introducing this marvel to Nonna. With no children to call her own, Nonna often smiled softly at the women in the marketplace with babes at their hips or toddlers with sticky hands. Kiri knew Nonna would delight in caring for him until his abilities could be properly assessed.

Circling the System's Main Entrance from above, Kiri pondered how best to get him inside without making a fuss. She decided there was nothing for it but to attempt to enter as usual and hope the guard on duty wasn't paying too much attention.

Swooping down, Kiri felt a sinking sensation that had little to do with their elevation change. Standing at attention in the mouth of the tunnel was Uto's companion, Buxton. Buxton was never *not* paying attention. In fact, he made a habit of questioning everyone attempting to enter the caves, even if he'd known them his whole life. He'd Bonded with Uto as a teenager, about a decade after Kiri's own Bonding ceremony. Now in his prime, he was every bit as rigid and pompous as he'd been as a child.

Kiri tensed her jaw as she landed on the edge of the cliff, bracing herself for the incoming nuisance. Inconveniently, the boy on her back began to cry again, the adrenaline catching up to him.

Buxton immediately flagged her down, raising his bracer-clad arm. "Ho!" He called, "Who goes there?"

Kiri longed to respond with something like, "Buxton, I remember when you wet your swaddling," but she supposed it was for the best that she couldn't speak. Instead, she radiated the signature impression of her identity, the only non-emotion dragons were able to emit.

Kiri, the Skin of the Forest, she sent, along with **impatience,** hoping he would allow her to just get the wailing child inside, away from the biting wind.

"Not so fast, now!" Buxton approached, eyes on the boy. He seemed to be attempting a jovial attitude, but Kiri knew him better than that.

He wasn't going to let this one slide. "Who's this little fellow?"

As Buxton came closer, the child gasped and immediately ceased his crying. Kiri realized he must remember the soldier from the attack. The boy stayed very still, as if Buxton would forget about him if he didn't make any sudden movements. Unfortunately, his fluffy winter garb did nothing to camouflage him against Kiri as her scales did to the trees.

Still, Buxton didn't seem to recognize the boy. Changing tactics, he motioned for the pair to follow him. "Come along," he said. "Uto's just inside. I'd rather have this conversation with everyone present."

Kiri's stomach sank further. She knew Uto would smell the smoke on him as easily as she had. He'd put the pieces together in no time. Kiri feared that Uto, with his volatile temper, would want to exterminate the child as quickly as he had the parents. She carefully kept her emotions private, however, not wanting to spook the boy.

She knew his best chance of survival was to show Uto what he could do. She only hoped he'd have the chance to.

Buxton led them through the main entrance to a stuffy cave where guards came to warm themselves between shifts. Here, the cave walls were void of any moisture, thanks to the roaring fire in the center of the room.

Uto was dropping a log onto the flames as the trio approached, unhinging his powerful jaws. He batted the sparks away with a flick of his tail and nudged the ventilation hood closer with a forepaw the size of a dinner plate.

Kiri swallowed, mentally comparing her apple-sized mitts with his impressive battle-sharpened claws. There wasn't much she could hope to do if things got violent.

"Uto, brother," Buxton drawled, leading them inside. "What make you of this stray Kiri's dragged in?"

Kiri felt the boy scramble off her back and attempt to duck behind her haunches. She glanced back at him before looking at Uto and sending **compassion,** trying to warn him off over-reacting.

96

Uto let out a sharp burst of air from his nostrils. Snaking his head past Buxton, he tasted the air next to the boy, who whimpered.

Rearing up, Uto snorted, emitting **frustration,** then recounting **success** and the **satisfaction** of a job well done. Or so he had thought.

"Leftovers from the battle this morning?" Buxton clarified. Uto blinked his confirmation.

"Just as I suspected," his companion boasted. Kiri again felt a surge of exasperation, knowing full well the soldier hadn't put the story together until Uto arranged the pieces. "Dispose of him."

Kiri growled at Buxton, placing herself between Uto and the boy. Turning to the child, she sent him **hope,** trying to encourage a response.

"Why waste your emotions on him?" Buxton criticized.

Kiri could feel the child trembling.

"It is not as if he comprehends what only us Bonded can experience."

At that, the boy's resolve seemed to harden. He used a hand on her leg to pull himself up to his full, albeit minuscule, height beside her.

Staring up into the soldier's eyes, he radiated **defiance**.

The room collectively inhaled. Time slowed to a stop, then sped up all at once.

Buxton shouted in alarm, calling for more guards and their soldiers. Uto roared, sweeping his tail across the room to trap them in the corner. Before Kiri could even consider retaliating, the room was full of a half dozen dragons in full armor.

Thus, she ended up on a bed of damp hay in a cell of the Prison Sector.

Mulling it over, she wished she had thought to enter through a side tunnel as if she'd hunted in the East by the lake, or along the southern canyon. But no, she had to go flying in the Main Entrance, stocked with the ranks of guards and battle-hungry soldiers.

They'd put the boy in the cell next to hers. Kiri sent him **remorse**.

He replied with **forgiveness**.

She hoped someone kind would tell Nonna where she was.

In the hours that followed, Kiri thought about what Nonna would do if she were here. She knew Nonna would attempt to comfort the boy, so Kiri poked her snout through the bars to rest on his lap. Nonna would make him laugh, so Kiri made shapes with her tail to cast silly shadows from the light of the lone torch. Nonna would offer him her food, but the guards left them nothing but water, so the rumbles of their bellies sounded in harmony against the cave walls.

As the hours turned into days, she began to worry he would starve. He slept a lot and would barely drink when she nudged the water bucket toward him. They heard not even whispers from the world above, isolated down the deepest hallway.

Kiri assumed Buxton had alerted the System Leaders, who now must be debating whether or not to keep the child alive or quietly kill him. He had every potential to influence the balance of power.

Humans were not known for willingly relinquishing power.

Late in the fourth night of their imprisonment, Kiri was keeping watch over the boy, as usual. She rested her snout on his chest, her tail wrapped around his sleeping form, the bars between their cells awkwardly keeping them apart. She was grateful he'd been so warmly dressed when she found him, as no one bothered to heat this sector just for the prisoners.

Kiri jerked her head up at the jangling sound of keys. She'd been ready to believe they'd decided to let them rot.

Footsteps echoed down the hall. Kiri blearily untangled herself from the bars and crouched before her gate, ready to bite off the head of whoever had deigned to come see them at last. Figuratively, of course. Maybe literally, if she got the chance. But as she caught sight of her visitor, all the fight left her body in one fell swoop.

Nonna crouched down, reaching her warm hands through the bars to cup Kiri's face. "My dearest Kiri," she whispered. "What have they done to you?"

Keening softly, Kiri nuzzled into Nonna's grip, pouring all her love into Nonna's palms. "Let's get you out of there," Nonna huffed, pulling back to sort through the keys on her belt.

Kiri blinked through her hunger and exhaustion, catching up to this turn of events. She sent **astonishment** and **curiosity** to Nonna as her cell gate clicked open.

Nonna quickly began work on the gate of the child's cell. "It's a long story," she grunted, lifting the hinge. "I'll tell it later."

Kiri accepted this answer, trusting Nonna implicitly. She wriggled in and nudged the boy awake. He stirred slowly at first but rapidly focused on the halo of Nonna's wiry curls.

"Hello," Nonna murmured, taking a knee beside him. "I'm Nonna. We're going to get you out of this place, okay?"

The boy nodded, emitting **gratitude**.

Nonna pulled in a breath. "There were rumors," she whispered. "His ability . . . I didn't believe . . ."

Eager to escape, Kiri crouched beside the child as she had once before. He gripped a spike and pulled himself up at once, understanding her urgency.

"The wine wagon is in the main prison passage," Nonna explained, a comforting hand on Kiri's neck. "Get yourself inside the barrels. They should be empty. I'm headed out the East Entrance to 'make a delivery.' Stay quiet. Got it?"

Both the boy and Kiri nodded. Nonna pressed a light kiss to Kiri's brow and stood up.

She pulled a dark hood over her hair, dampening the silver shimmering in the torchlight as she strode down the hall. Kiri scampered behind her.

Glancing both ways at the end of the hall, Nonna confidently approached her wagon, patting the mule on his flank. Mounting the oak buckboard, she gathered the reigns with a practiced hand.

Kiri stuck to the shadows, passing a soldier snoring loudly in a chair. The sweet stench of wine surrounded him. There was a suspicious lack of keys at his belt. Kiri looked to Nonna, who winked and motioned to the bed of the wagon.

The barrels were positioned perfectly to allow a small boy to crawl into one and a small dragon to squeeze into another. Not daring to emote in the passage, in case any Bonded soldiers lurked nearby, Kiri kept her unending gratitude to herself. She hoped Nonna knew how she felt anyway.

Kiri used her tail to flip the edge of the canvas cover over the barrels, throwing the two of them into darkness. Around them, she noticed several other barrels that, by the smell of them, were certainly not filled with wine. Grain in one, wool in another, some collection of metals in that last one . . . What did Nonna have planned?

As they trundled along in the dark, the sounds of the System grew louder with each corner they turned. They left the Prison Sector behind, hurrying through the System Official caves, then trundled through a residential sector. Kiri knew they were driving through the marketplace when the scent of cured meats made her mouth water. Not far now until the East Entrance.

They joined the queue to exit the System. Kiri could hear Nonna chatting with fellow tradespeople as they approached the guards, spinning her tale as well as she spun the wool for her blankets.

"Yes, Kiri's still away on her hunting trip," Nonna lied, commiserating with a blacksmith. "Got to do the deliveries all by my lonesome."

An Official at the exit finally stopped her. "What's all this, then?"

"A half dozen wine barrels for the duchess of the lake," Nonna simpered. "Such a loyal customer."

The Official let her through with no further trouble.

Unable to believe their luck, Kiri fought to stay still and quiet until the clatter of the system and nearby wagons had completely faded away.

Nonna reached back and rapped her knuckles on a barrel. "Come on out, dears. We're in the clear."

Kiri slunk out of her barrel, muscles cramped. She fumbled with the canvas until it snapped back, blinking in the bright rays of the early morning.

The sky was a pale blue, crystalline in beauty after her days in prison. She hopped to the front to curl around Nonna's frail frame, overwhelming her with a wave of emotions.

Nonna just wrapped her arm around Kiri and laughed. "You know I'd do absolutely anything for you, darling." She dug around in her knapsack. "Here, give the boy some bread. There's a waterskin in here as well. And, oops!" She fumbled the rations as the wagon hit a frost heave in the cobbled road. "There's salted venison in a barrel out back."

Kiri gently grasped the supplies between her teeth, careful not to puncture the waterskin. She reached her neck back to face the child. He was still curled in his barrel, reluctant to emerge.

As she had when they first met, she sent him **calm** and **comfort**, coaxing him out with the offering of food. He clambered to the front bench to sit between Nonna and Kiri, clutching the bread as if it were going to fly away.

"Go on," encouraged Nonna. "Slowly now, or you'll make yourself sick."

Kiri curled her tail around his waist to keep him from jostling about too much with the motion of the wagon. As she watched him eat, a small blossom of warmth spread in her chest. It felt good to see him recovering, to be able to provide the care he'd been desperately lacking. Their time in prison had made her oddly protective over him, she realized. He didn't seem so repulsive, nothing like how she regarded the sticky-fingered children of the System.

Shaking herself from her revere, she looked to Nonna and emitted **curiosity** again.

Nonna grinned. "What I told the Official wasn't too far off. I do have a delivery for the estate of the duchess of the lake. But what the Official doesn't know, because I'm sure Buxton has covered his tracks thoroughly, is that the duchess of the lake is recently deceased. She was inside a humble carriage in a wagon train Uto mistook for bandits. The duchess left her entire estate to her firstborn son, the very boy who sits between us now."

The boy looked up from his bread. "Mama?" he asked, his voice reaching Kiri's ears for the first time like the song of a finch.

Nonna placed her hand atop his knitted cap. "I'm so sorry, honey. But we're going to get you home now."

The boy seemed to contemplate this news, then nodded, breaking off a piece of his bread and offering it to Nonna.

She accepted the morsel, giving him a soft smile. "You never told us your name. What are you called?"

He looked between the two of them, then grinned. Both with his voice and his heart, he told them his name, emitting his signature identity.

"Doryu!"

Kiri felt the truth of who he was vibrate through her bones as understanding cleared the wrinkles from Nonna's brow.

"Doryu," she repeated. "One Who Understands the Ways of Dragons."

Kiri raised her head and trumpeted at the sky. She could think of no better companions to break away from the System with. They were heading somewhere not even Uto and Buxton could bury them under layers of bureaucracy, somewhere far away, somewhere safe.

As long as they were together, they were heading home.

Selected poems
by Amber Grell

The Void

Time is flying by
since the last time you
saw me
kissed me
   missed me

The moon rises
and falls
faster than it ever has
and it's scary to see all this
time
breaking
up
what we had

i just want you to be
here

and i know i'm the reason

you aren't.

months, years, decades
will go by
and I'll still be reaching
for a sign
for you

to come back
mistakes make any gap bigger
mine made ours infinite

Untitled

That's the worst way for something to end
—in your hands

When someone else breaks your heart
you get over it
It may take months
or years
but eventually you'll move on
because they gave you that definitive clarity
that a "what if" doesn't exist

But when you break someone else's heart
and later
regret
it

You'll never get over it
You'll never forgive yourself

It'll be thirty-five years later
and you'll still wake up every day
wishing for him
wanting him
laying next to someone else
wondering why you broke both of you

It's a mistake that will never leave
It lingers in every waking moment
and in so many dreams

It's worse to break his heart
because he won't take you back
and you'll have to live each day knowing
you
are the cause of your own unhappiness

You

You can't blame anyone this time
You can only blame yourself

Congrats.

ABC

A day ago I didn't feel like this.

Broken and cheap.

Catastrophe floods my veins like sleet on a busy night.

Does it matter that I didn't even want this?

Even though my heart will tell you long lies otherwise—

Figures, it's always betraying me—

Ghosts tell it secrets through the night.

Have you ever wondered what makes people disappear?

I do.

Just when things are blossoming, the heat wave comes in, trashing everything.

Kleptomaniacs make sense to me—starting the world on fire.

Losing everything on purpose.

Magic.

Nothing remains this way. No trail in sight. Nothing to latch onto.

One way to make something go away is to completely destroy it.

People will hold onto even the slightest shred of hope, a piece of paper, a memory, a feeling.

Quietly listen.

Rain will come after the fire to vanish the remnants.

Skies will eventually clear.

Then you can start picking something fresh.

Under every storm is a day that follows.

Vanquish the old.

Welcome the new.

Zealously.

Safe Haven

my heart is as

                      still

     as the water

before me

like a red carpet

welcoming me

to the

                      city

the buildings

making up a beautiful

        game

of tetris

each placed

perfectly

       in line

i follow the path

one foot after the other

gliding on

      crimson

passing greenery

as leaves clear the path

      ahead of me

until i enter the party

        welcomed

New York

tears slide down as the lights turn off around the city
tonight.

But,

there's something so serene about sitting in Times Square
alone

    crying

people pass and notice

but they're all hurting inside, too

instead of passing with judgment,

they silently nod in acknowledgement.

New York is a compilation of abandoned people searching
for something

more

we all smile in amazement of the city surrounding us

but the smiles hide how

broken

and

afraid

we feel

                              engulfed in the lights

millions of strangers huddled together towards dreams

hoping to stay warm

in the long battle towards

                                    the end

is it ever the "end", though?

no matter what we accomplish

or who we become

we are never satisfied

*when did the fight for "more" become superior to the fight for
happiness?*

I Used to Think

I Used to Think
That I was weak.
That equality was inevitable.
That people could be selfless.
That work could be fulfilling.
That money wasn't important.
That boyfriends were a priority.
That fate had a way of carrying itself.
That fairytales existed.
That love was romantic.
That he was The One.

And now I don't.

If You See the Shell That's Left of Me
by Kaitlyn Keel

He hadn't meant for it to get this bad, but God, his sinuses hurt. He sneezed, and then again, before refilling the humidifier next to his bed. He'd just gotten his nose to stop bleeding again, the skin above his mustache aching and dry from the constant rubbing.

He grabbed the Vaseline from his nightstand, rubbing the thick gel over his dry skin on his face before he climbed back into his bed. The sheets scratched at his skin, a smell emanating from them. He couldn't remember the last time he had washed them.

Frankie sighed, glancing at the bag of coke sitting on his nightstand. He glanced away just as quickly, ashamed of himself.

It was only meant to be recreational, something to take the edge off after he got shot the second time. He needed something to escape the thoughts, the demons.

He had it all under control, until he didn't.

The cravings increased tenfold once he got out. The nightmares had gotten worse, plaguing his sleep every night.

A therapist diagnosed him with PTSD and gave him some kind of medication for the anxiety and something for his sleep, but Frankie was impatient. He wasn't willing to wait a few weeks for the medicine to work through his system, he needed relief now.

At first, it was a couple of lines a week, something to take the edge off and keep him awake so he wouldn't have to face his demons.

He tried to quit a few times over the next few years, once even using vacation days at work to put himself in a treatment center. But he always went back, surrendering to the high.

Someone reported him at work. Who it was, he had no idea. He only did lines at home, never while on the clock. And yeah, maybe he was high a few times on a shift, but he never compromised anyone's safety.

They ran a drug test, and that was that. The FAA suspended him, took his pilot's license, pending review.

He'd dug himself into a hole with no way out.

He no longer had a reason to leave the house, so he didn't, unless he was meeting with his dealer. He stayed in bed most of the time, blackout curtains closed. He barely ate, almost always takeout. He couldn't remember the last time he went to the grocery store or whether he'd taken a shower that week.

All he knew was the coke.

§

A continuous knock rang out, waking Jo from a deep slumber. Groaning, she sat up and took a look at the clock.

4:04 a.m.

Who was knocking on her door at four a.m.

She slid out of bed, searching for her slippers in the dark. The floor was cold, making her shiver as she walked around her bedroom. When she couldn't find them, she sighed, pulling on her robe to meet whoever was at the door.

But when she swung open the door, she wasn't expecting her best friend to be the cause of the noise. "Frankie?"

Frankie pushed past her, walking into her apartment while he muttered to himself. He looked like hell. Eyes bloodshot, dry blood crusted under his nose from a nosebleed, hair damp from sweat. He smelled disgusting, as if he hadn't showered in days.

He walked around her apartment aimlessly, hands tugging at his hair. "*Girasol*, I love you." He looked at her then, tired brown eyes peering at her own.

"I love you too, *mi amor*. What's going on?" She took a step toward him, but he took a step back. She held her hands up in a quiet surrender, searching for answers on his face.

"Frankie?"

"No, you don't understand. I love you; I'm in love with you. We . . . we can go to Mexico right now, like I promised. We can get married, just like we talked about when we were kids." He rambled on, spewing memories that brought only pain to her.

112

"Frankie, what are you doing here?"

He walked over to her and fell to his knees in front of her frame, hands gravitating to her hips. "Marry me."

"Francisco, this isn't funny. Get up," she muttered, trying to pull him off the ground.

"Funny? I'm not jokin', cariño. Please," he begged, hands pulling away from her body to dig through his pockets. "I'm sure I've got something . . ."

Frankie froze as a bag of white powder fell from his hands. The room stood still as the coke hit the floor of her living room, silencing him. Her eyes widened, the realization hitting her. The man in front of her was suffering far deeper than she could have imagined.

Within seconds, she sprang into action. She lowered herself to the ground in front of him, holding his head gently in her hands. "Let's get you in the shower, yeah?"

He nodded slightly, and she grabbed his arm, tugging him up and then down the hall to the bathroom. She sat Frankie down on the toilet and reached to turn on the shower head so it could heat up while she worked.

She grabbed a towel from the hall closet before digging through her dresser for some of Frankie's old clothes. He hadn't worn the shirt or sweats in years, but Jo hoped they would still fit him.

When she returned to the bathroom, Frankie was still sitting on the toilet, staring silently at the wall in front of him. She sat everything down on the counter before making her way to stand in front of him.

Jo tugged his shirt off gently, whispering thank yous with every movement. She helped him stand, undoing his shoes and removing his socks before she moved to his pants.

"You're going so great, Frankie. We're almost there."

He made a small noise of acknowledgment, holding onto Jo's shoulders for balance as she helped remove his pants and boxers.

She'd seen him naked years ago, when things were simpler between them, but Jo averted her eyes as best she could to keep a semblance of privacy. Once finished, she helped him into the tub and under the warm water flowing from the shower head. Placing a washcloth into his hands, she pressed a light kiss to his cheek before pulling the curtain back.

"Call for me if you need help, okay?"

"Thank you," Frankie mumbled, almost inaudible over the sound of the shower.

Jo then quietly slipped out of the bathroom, closing the door gently behind her. She leaned against the wall next to the door, knees giving out as she slid to the ground. Her head fell into her hands as she crumbled, body shaking with sobs.

A Year Ago Tomorrow You Died

by Shannon Huurman

A year.
How can it be a year
when I've yet to breathe?
My shoulders
have not settled.
My eyes still red and puffy.
I think of us
making plans to travel Europe on your front porch
swing
after I graduated college.
Did you know then you would die before I could cross
the stage?
And do you know that
I've not yet brought myself to
go back and sit on your porch swing.
The moon got smaller
and larger,
twelve times over.
The days got shorter
and now they get longer,
but not one has passed
where you have not
lived in my brain.

Two a.m.
by Shannon Huurman

I was lying in bed,
thinking of you,
When suddenly I heard a
train horn blaring.
"How strange,"
I thought.
I didn't even know the train
ran through here.

you make me the purplest
by Kimberly Anderson

your jeep wrangles my
hair as we drive top-down
through the sea canyon—
tangy malibu air dances
with the dead space that lingers
between our magnetic, clammy
palms and the glistening june sun
kisses my skin in a way that
only a lover does.
you careen down
searing asphalt roads
like you know me already.
and i'm lucky:

you said you like me best
when i'm wildly untamed yet
perfectly radiant, optimistic
but still ready for a storm.

god, i wish i could freeze
this moment
so i could live
for

one

second

longer.

Girl
After "Wife" by Ada Limon
by Kimberly Anderson

I think it will take a long time before
I am comfortable with the word that
sounds like a clean break but is actually a
pre-written eulogy. The one where
inspiration is crushed into the sidewalk and
all that is left is estranged chalk dust
married to the fleeting wind. Whisked away
to the place where all dreams go. The
word that is tossed between one uncle and
another when a mother's opening is
stretched and stressed, then they all scream,
"It's a girl!"
Girl, why does it sound like
unfurl? A word disguised as dying
light. Like when the sun goes down,
and the moon becomes a false substitute.
A girl that plays, pretends, fits in—
but not too much. That forgets and
submits. That looks and loves in one direction.
That paints over dimmed moonlight with
shades of fuchsia and blush so Mommy
can get a good picture. And then I remember
that all words have endings. I remember that
this one does not. I remember that I was too
much of a girl—

and yet not enough of one.

Blank Me

by Kimberly Anderson

I.

Soft raindrops grip the screen that separates my
    cruel room from the chattering sky.
    My mother's feet

    pound down our shared hallway while I'm
suffocating behind thin walls. The once-fluffy clouds and I
mourn our shared pain.

II.

I often wonder what it would be like to wear a face without
needing to take it off at bedtime or live
    without worrying about what words

    may stumble out of my mother's mouth or not
apologize to people who don't understand the word *love* but

I cannot really answer these things because I always fear
the
    moment that someone might say
    "I _____ you."

III.

I used to love rain. Rain was a hug—a tight hug. On the
    good days, rain might embrace me faster than my

    mother could. Rain also becomes a rainbow. I used
to smile at rainbows but now all those colors remind me of
people I can't

say *"I love you"* to in an open room.

A Portrait for Healing

by Kimberly Anderson

Draw me a portrait, Mama.
Draw me with light
in my eyes and passion
between my teeth,

but only color me in
shades of purple.

Don't change the
things you once
hated, like my
unruly hair and
lingering fingers.

Don't erase my heart,
though it confuses you;
I know there are people
you want me to love
that I can't find
my way to.

Please don't make me
forget who I am, to fill a
void of the girl you
thought you once knew.

Retreat to me.
Learn me again.

Go back to a time when I ran,
and you followed,

to a time when the
color of my heart
didn't matter,

to a time when love was
the only emotion
between us.

Draw me with warmth in
your heart and inspiration
on the tip of your tongue
Mama,

& let me grow that way.

My Blue Ribbon

by Jack Niemczyk

Sullivan Street. Rain. An October in New York City. The type of day that causes you to roll your eyes as if it could be any more archetypal. An ambiance that is so perfect that I walk with an air of caution for fear that I may just meet my Hallmark man waiting under an awning, smoking a cigarette and softly humming a Chet Baker song. A day like this causes me to be nothing but *shivers* happy. "Odd," I observe, how the rain pattering against my buttery leather jacket, ruining my *vintage veste* with every thump, can make a person feel lonely and yet whole. Leaves crunch under my boots to underscore the throaty genius of Billie Holiday that rings in my ears as *Heaven* finally enters my vision.

The Blue Ribbon Brasserie—a restaurant opened in the 90s to satisfy the seediest of individuals: chefs. This culinary chapel, known for keeping its doors open until 4 a.m., became a hub for all who worked the grueling schedule of the restaurant industry. It provided a hard drink, good food, and an eclectic crowd of like-minded charlatans that included the likes of Anthony Bourdain, Andrew Zimmern, and my parents. On a gloomy Tuesday at 6 p.m. I stroll into the restaurant that was once brimming with the best of the culinary underbelly of New York, but now services self-proclaimed "foodies" hoping to catch a glimpse of something . . . anything. But this restaurant has a special place in my imagination as the spot that will host the first date to conclude the long grueling course of homosexuality, but today, in existence, I am alone.

I've never been afraid to go to a restaurant alone. Growing up in restaurants, whether it be the one my mother piloted or the one my father silently commanded, I always felt at home among the white tablecloths and polished cutlery. They were an extension of my room. My parents never permitted their parenthood to interfere with their experience at a nice restaurant. Even as a toddler, when I became cranky they would simply push two chairs together to form a makeshift cot, lay me down, and enjoy their curated charcuterie board—always nudging me awake for a drowsy taste of the stinky cheese that joined us at the table.

My family has always been defined by food. Upon finishing college my mother pursued culinary school— not just any culinary school but the Culinary Institute of America in Hyde Park, New York. Quite the journey for the spunky girl who spent her whole life in Florida. She had yet to be accepted to the school or determine how and where she would stay in Hyde Park, but her mind was made. She promptly went to her boyfriend at the time and simply said, "I'm going to culinary school; you're either coming with me or you aren't." My father replied prosaically, as if they were discussing the weather, "Give me two weeks." Not 14 days later they loaded their Gainesville life into a busted '89 pickup truck and began plodding along I-95.

97 Sullivan Street. The alluring navy door groans open as I remove my jacket. Filled with spite, the jacket decided to dribble the droplets of rain directly on my crotch. I stand looking at my root chakra that is now drenched in God's tears and sigh. "No matter," I think, as I flippantly swing my coat over my left arm and give it a smack on the bum—a small retaliation. I look up and my eyes meet with a woman, glowing like a candle struggling to keep its wick upright. Her face was familiar, like the English teacher at everyone's school who would so often favor the closeted homosexual, and no one really ever knew why? Kind and damaged, with stringy dyed blonde hair that gripped me with fear for my future and blue eyes that apologized before they struck. She is the guardian of the establishment, the Saint Peter of these hallowed walls. I see her every time I frequent this sacred place. "I wonder if she remembers me," I think as we exchange platitudes. I have a face that is not often forgotten. People cannot help but stare, often gawking at me like an intricate sword used to assassinate some old white guy: beautiful, but apparent that I could strike at any moment.

The *maître d'* ushers me to the bar, suggesting that I would be happiest there as a party of one. While she isn't wrong, it still stings. A fuzzy wink reveals deep blue eyeshadow, otherwise hidden by her hooded eyes, providing an ointment for the sting. "HELLO?" My liver beckons to me, asking for a drink in the most masochistic way. No one seems to be servicing libations, but as I look down the infinite mahogany bar, I see the bartender making his way up a ladder that is begging for an OSHA violation. He welcomes me, his *enchanté* like hot apple cider, releasing a warmth throughout my body and causing tears to create pressure behind my eyes. Not because I am sad, but because his fervor is exactly what was needed. I respond, flirtatiously of course. His cobalt eyes are stronger than that of the *maître d'* and are akin to a pool that is perfectly cool. When the water is as smooth as silk, cooling and caressing every inch of your submerged skin. The type of water that yearns for you to bask in it—not for fun, but for some kind of sensual pleasure. My crescent smile begins the descent into that darkness as the rest of his visage comes into view. He looks as if the Snuggle® laundry detergent bear did ketamine and lived in Bushwick: exactly my type.

> My mother completed culinary school while my father
> spread his genius about staging in restaurants, working
> as a professor at CUNY, and training as a sommelier
> in the city. After several blissfully childless years
> they made the journey due South and headed back to
> Florida. Once again, they deepened the path of I-95,
> retracing the steps that gifted them those wonderful
> years of their life, to start a family. However, they were
> careful as to not fall down the rabbit hole that so many
> fledgling parents do after children are introduced to
> the picture. They both stayed true to their culinary
> roots, my mom as part of a catering company and my
> father as a sommelier at a fine dining steakhouse. My
> mother, as she was prone, sought out more. She soon
> opened her own restaurant, *Family Meal*, which was
> embraced by our community and became a local staple.
> At this point they had a daughter and an angelic,
> hilarious, surprisingly-sexy-for-his-age son (yes, it is
> me and no, the description is not dramatized). Almost
> every day after school, I was whisked away to help my
> mother around the restaurant or do my homework
> behind a golden bar, listening to my father lust about
> fermented grapes. He described his wine pairings as
> a love affair, and it was the closest thing to the birds

and the bees I ever got. "When a prawn and a Riesling love each other very much . . ." and so forth. Although rather unconventional, moments like those defined my kinder years.

And even as my parents pivoted career paths and their culinary expertise was limited to use around the house, the quality never waned. Each night a different cuisine, a different preparation, a different wine pairing. My sister and I were often allowed a sip of wine to complement our meal—not to be sloshing over—but to see how fermented grapes are akin to a necklace with an evening gown. The dress is good and easily palatable, but the jewels transport the look to a different galaxy. Each and every meal was wonderful, but I learned from an early age the true seal of approval—when a meal was simply so delicious, my father would turn into the likes of Homer Simpson and emit a cartoonish "ughh" as if he had just savored his first donut. That noise was the gastronomic euphoria I sought out but never managed to find.

He taunts me with a drink. "Well, I already have a tall glass of water." I say. Humiliating. I mean royally humiliating. He laughs with the charity of Mother Teresa and says he has something in mind for me. He returns with a wine glass, filled to the brim thanks to my desperate attempt at being friendly. He places the glass in front of me, a deep burgundy liquid that shakes its supple curves as I lift the thin glass to my lips . . . ecstasy. A 2009 Côtes du Rhône filled my mouth with the sundrenched grapes of Eastern France. Its plump plum flavor greeted my taste buds with a pinch and the tannins tickled my molars on the way down. My eyes open again, and he greets me with the misty shoreline and nods, "Right?" As the tannins continue their tap-dance I place my order—the sole reason I came here. "**Beef Marrow & Oxtail Marmalade**," even as I speak the words my mouth begins to water.

Growing up in a house that worshiped the culinary gods more than the theological ones warranted exactly what one might expect: a wealth of knowledge about food. Despite their respective full-time jobs my parents

125

cooked every night. Over dinner we conversed about the meal and subsequently contemplated the following day's menu. Upon vacation, we would rack up bills in the thousands for the sheer celebration of sustenance. My family was never affectionate; I was taught that food was the ultimate love language. Undoubtedly, we appeared more hardened than the average family, but our unity solidified when we could sit together and partake at the dinner table—our safe haven. Only there could we release all of our burdens as we primitively cracked and shattered stone crab, claw after claw, mangling it as we slurped up the buttery bliss that lay within its tender meat. The essence of such gustatory pleasures placed a crustacean band-aid on any woe we faced in the outside world. My father's subsequent "ughh" always followed a meal like this. I did always wonder though, as I spent time with my friends' parents, why mine never seemed to poke and prod and hug and embrace in the way theirs did. It never bothered me per se but was an interesting case study for my young mind.

The dish is soon bestowed upon me. I warn the bartender for fear that in this brief period when the dish is in sight I may salivate at an egregious rate. He puts out the wet floor sign. The aroma hits me before its picture. Any dryness caused by the season's change has now become moisturized. The smell can only be described in one way: happiness. The pristine dish is adorned with a blue ribbon to match its namesake. A thin gold leaf hugs the plate and frames the reverent image in front of me. Oxtail marmalade, red and wanton, sits adjacent to brioche clouds, plump with a morning dew of homemade butter. And the pièce de résistance, four ridged veal bones teeming with the elixir of the gods.

My parents always say how food is a time capsule; how flavors capture and preserve our clearest memories. The first taste transports me back two years, back to when I was a bone marrow virgin. My family was

126

visiting me for the first time since moving to New York and their presence was already warm enough. My parents sang praises of the good old days of this establishment, drinking with fellow iconoclasts until the early hours of the morning before making their way back upstate. Up to this point, I had appreciated food—loved it even—but never enough to match their verdant adoration. But in that moment, as my lips opened to receive that first bite, everything I thought I knew about food changed. My eyes shut and pyrotechnics erupted behind them. All the colors on the plate liquified and melded together behind the dark of my eyelids. Tears entered my closed eyes and the only comprehensible sound to match the symphony in my mouth erupted from my throat: "Ughh." In a rush, I saw every scratch on my knee that warranted buttery mashed potatoes and every A+ on my report card that was rewarded with lobster and home-clarified butter. Not in the adages that were half thrown out, but in the beauty that was created on my plate. I realized I would never want it any other way; a hug is a moment, but a meal is a memory. It was perfect as it was, perfect in its edible ways.

I dig into the sizzling plate sitting in front of me, carving into the gelatinous center and loading it onto the supple brioche. As my eyes close and mouth opens I feel a familiar hug: the love that a stranger infused into this dish in 54 laborious hours. My body melts into the wooden barstool and any notion of loneliness is flushed out of my body, cleansed with this bite, and subsequently polished off by the wine. My eyes lazily open, like those mornings you forget to set an alarm and wake up later than intended, a moment of true peace before chaos ensues. The surf and his infectious smile welcome me back to earth. I lounge in the pool of his eyes with the knowledge that many patrons will never understand and offer him a bite. He accepts and, as our jaws synchronize, we shoot to a different dimension—one that is just a warm blanket of light. We call this place home for just a few beatific moments before the patron behind me drops her glass. He tops off mine, free of charge, and we talk about food. I share my story, proud of the fact that I can still feel the warm embrace of my family in my molars.

I enjoy every last bite chatting with the bartender. He's a very lovely person who is unfortunately cursed with heterosexuality, but we all have our flaws. I pay the bill and say goodnight to his coastal tide pool for a while. I nod to the chef who peaks his head out for a second; perhaps he thinks I am simply another peon, but I know I am more. I am a lineage of food, a product of the love that food has brought forth. I bid adieu to the bright blue *maître d'* who is not apologizing as she had before. I walk back down Sullivan Street, heading uptown. Gazing up Sixth Ave, the building seems to split perfectly down the middle, and the dark cerulean sky with its flecks of pink and purple is completely unobstructed. The toothpick I snagged as a memento dislodges a forgotten piece of marrow, holding onto my tooth for dear life. The memory once again sends shivers down my body, and I can feel a warmth that even a dryer set to "hot" could not muster; a warmth that encompasses the hurt and joy and madness of my life. Mine is a life that may constitute eating alone in a New York restaurant and flirting with a hetero, but I am home in my mind. I taste my successes and know that my family is proud of me. They may not present me with the standard blue ribbon that reflects the mediocrity in everyone else's minor accomplishments, but rather with my Blue Ribbon . . . and it's a damn tasty one.

A Successive Issue

by Jack Niemczyk

"What happened to straight people being straight people?" I muse as my weakened gin and tonic flows down my throat. This watered-down mixture provides the smallest amount of comfort in an environment more consecutive in nature than I had hoped for. *What happened to homosexuality in New York City?* Surrounded by mullets, painted nails, and shiny loafers—the wayfinding points that used to alleviate this issue of romance, now camouflaged within a trend. Pursuing the organisms in the room. Eye-contact. Lacking thought but brimming with lust. Sauntering to the pool table, playing with the balls (ironic). He poses the game; doubles? No, singles (thank God). Janis Joplin wails her piquant tone as we begin our game. One of billiards, of course, but more so one of Love and Lust, the hardest game to play in a city as aromantic as this. *thunk* I'm stripes, he's solid (it writes itself). Kansas City? (Friend of Dorothy?) Talking of the smallest things in nature. My eyes only able to focus on his lips, tender and slightly chapped, spewing lust and magnetizing my gaze. Avoiding depth and following with a joke. Winning both games thus far, I've needed this. We laugh, drink, and exchange casualties, occasionally a friendly hit on the arm, stinging as my touch-deprived skin yearns for another exchange. The game continues; warmth in my chest, he grins at me and sings my praises. Tied on the 8, now the game really begins. Will he ask to continue our conversation? Will we end in a handshake or perhaps a side hug? This odd litmus test that most non-city folk don't understand, but a crucial study of human behavior for me. A wink, I'm ruined. Falling for a stranger with a simple gesture. Be optimistic, perhaps the best will happen. He scratches the 8, Jesus. The worst way to win is by default. He warms my side, claiming "good game" and fulfilling me with the promise, "My girlfriend would love you." I agree with the knowledge that yes, she probably would, who doesn't love me? . . . *Who doesn't love me?* What happened to straight people being straight people?

City Sestina

by Jack Niemczyk

Mouth stings as I sip my martini,

I try to look cool as I sip, praying for the slight chaser
of lemon.

"With a twist," as per usual in my life.

Still, the drink's prickle warms my heart.

My mind races as it writes my cerebral novel.

On the cover, and in my vision, the full moon.

Odd how often she changes, this moon.

Its pull, like the tide, controlling the levels of my
martini.

"I am alone, what if I wasn't?" an idea so novel.

But the fear of rejection stings my wounds like a
lemon.

And what wound is greater than that of the heart?

But C'est La Vie!: something, something, LIFE!

I look out and see my course like a board game,
perhaps *The Game of Life*.

Its colorful spinner spun by the rising and setting of
the moon.

Its crescent warming my masochistic heart.

"Another round" shouts the fluted glass that once held
my martini.

I shout to the waiter, who replies with the acidic tinge
of a lemon.

And once again I begin to write this clairvoyant novel.

I look over, another joins me at the bar, a boy who looks like he jumped out of a novel.

His cheeks flushed with the red promise of life.

And his hair, a light yellow, shimmering out of his hat like the rind of a lemon.

His eyes pitch black like the slight moment when the sun eclipses the moon.

He asks what I'm drinking, "martini",

I say dryly. This nuanced pun warming my heart.

Chatting, moving closer, I can hear his heart.

It thumps, like the closing of a cover as you finish a novel

he welcomes his olive martini

Placing his hand on mine, advancing this game of life.

My intuition leaves, jumping away like a cow over the moon

I take a swig, hoping he's not another lemon.

Could he be flirting, could I take this chance? Well, when life gives you a lemon

Make lemonade, squeeze this plump juice with the ridges of your heart

And pass it through the phases of the moon

To make a liquid SO refreshing its idea becomes overused in a YA novel

A novel that shows the beauty of life

I finish my martini

Could it be till morning or till he finished his martini, will he be sweet or sour like that lemon?

This is the beauty of life, he could be forever or just something I feel sometimes in my heart

I hope to continue this novel, and that our story won't close, eclipse like the moon.

The Modern-Day Ghazal

by Jack Niemczyk

Modern-day ghazal strays from the ideas of love, loss,
and alcohol. Put that in your bin
"I haven't shit to write then", I begin my second
negroni, pouring the gin

Love. Loss. And Alcohol, I think. The masochistic triad
always looms over me, poking like a pin
laughing at my misfortune from just another table as
they clink their tonic and gin

The affair surrounds all decisions in life. But in the
ghazal, we must stray like its mortal sin
Must stray, though the thought always on my mind
until I taste that herbaceous gin

Loss. Love. They sit perfectly cruel, often near each
other always akin
a malevolent couplet of words that sting, flowery yet
spiced like an imported gin

A lost love, a time forgotten, yet we fill in
how can one forget a thing that never happened? The
answer lies in the rhyme scheme

Campari stains my finger, red and transferring to my
chin:
a cheap valentine's decoration, a loss of blood, a
negroni with gin

Love, Loss, Alcohol. This may not be a modern-day ghazal, and yet with a grin

who the hell cares, mama needs love, loss, and of course gin

This isn't a tale of rebellion, but one of submission, seeing it all cave in

As the liquid volume decreases, I see how I stray, thanking the gin

A cause of isolation. I often stray toward sin,

away from a modern-day ghazal, and toward love, loss, and gin

Why bother? Why care? The contemptuous couplet of loss and love, playing like a sad violin

its chorus will repeat again, again, a gin . . . another gin!

Yet I bother, and what do I get? Nothing but turmoil like East Berlin

Jack shit is all! And yet love and loss stay together,

the modern ghazal still broke, and still, I'm pouring the gin.

Through the Storm

by James Brandon Fizer

"I think David might be funny now," she had said out of nowhere while I was fixing her lunch plate. It was on one of my mid-day trips home recently to drop off her lunch without ever eating my own. "You know, mens sometimes mess with each other," she'd added. I already knew my son was gay, but it was rather surprising to realize someone her age would still pick up on it. And then bring it up, as if there were anything I could do about it. I'm sure that I had sighed, was hungry and irritable—no, exasperated—and probably said something like, "I'm sure David ain't thinking about what neither you nor I think about what he does in his private life." And on the way back to the shop I had wondered what kind of encounters she had had with gay men or men on the down-low in her long life. Something about, *You know, mens sometimes mess with each other*, and the idea that she thought she might be teaching me something new, made me think less about my son than, say, her husband, my grandfather. Then again, he was a notorious womanizer. I drove back to the shop that day wondering about the things she knew about the world and thought maybe I at 50 didn't already know.

She was always saying *something*. "You wearing a wig again or is that yours?" was her backhanded way of complimenting me on a new hairstyle. "You better put you on some sick weight," was her way of acknowledging that I had dropped a couple of pounds in the places that black women are wont to carry. I never knew what kind of unsolicited pronouncements to expect from her on these lunch drops. And yet oddly, when I was home at the end of the day and there was plenty of time to broach all kinds of subjects, she would retreat to her bedroom alone to watch game shows, prime-time soap operas, and read her Bible. Suddenly, resolving my son's sexuality or how I looked wasn't so interesting when I didn't have to rush out the door.

I knew she did it on purpose. It was her way of making sure I took some of her with me back to my day outside the house. Perhaps this is how old people spite you for leaving them alone all day. Leaving you with something to think about and carry with you since they couldn't go out themselves.

Then again, my grandmother has never been a nice woman, but she was a good woman. She worked hard. She raised my father to become a good man who was also a nice man. She nursed her husband throughout his failing later years long after he had finished beating her, cheating on her, drinking and cussing at her.

Mary is her name. At 98 years old, she has seen Jim Crow, the Great Depression, the Civil Rights Movement, and the upward mobility of her only child and grandchildren up north here in Detroit, Michigan, where my father moved after the war as part of the Great Migration. She would later move up here with the rest of us after losing most of her siblings. And then my father and my mother up here. Me, my three siblings, and her great-grandchildren were the remains of her line and she wanted to spend her final years with us. After my sister Aileen tried and failed to live with her in the house we grew up in, I put her in a nursing home and commenced taking her food daily and keeping her company for an hour. After a few years of a taxing commute that included multiple extra errands, including one in which my car was broken into outside the facility, I moved her into my house, against the advice of every single person I know. She was ornery, imperious, and authoritarian, but it was a hell of a lot easier than leaving someone under the dryer at my shop for an extra 45 minutes because I had to run out and pick my grandmother up some lunch.

"I'm so sick of you," she had told me once.

"Well, you better hope I don't get sick of *you*," is how I talked back to her. This is how we got along but, again, it was more convenient. Plus, how much longer could she live, anyway? Here I was, pre-menopausal, the mother of a young adult son who, like his generation, still often needed my financial assistance, taking care of my grandmother who sometimes talked to me like I were a child myself, and who could be as lucid as someone my age one minute, and then convinced that Pat Sajak was talking only to her when she got dressed up to watch *Wheel of Fortune* the next. At nearly a century old, she drank Busch beer out of a can every night, fried chicken from KFC every day, and went to church every Sunday, dressed to meet the Lord himself.

"They didn't have no original recipe thighs today?" she could scoff. There was absolutely nothing that you could slip by her. Not her change for a case of Busch or a bucket of chicken, not the amount of time she expected me to be at her side, not how much money she kept in her drawers with her underclothes.

But sometimes she told stories, long stories, and we would sit up for hours into the night and her memory was so immaculate and her tales so poignant and painful that I would weep and fall asleep absolutely in love with my grandmother. For her strength and perseverance, if not her kindness. After her life, who could expect her to be kind? And after my own taste of a drinking, violent husband, raising a black boy to manhood all on my own, and a demanding career as a stylist and beauty shop owner, I had a reputation of being a b-word myself. So I didn't need her to be a sweet old lady like the kind of woman my sweet, even docile, stay-at-home mother was.

Like my grandmother, I too have been through some storms.

After her husband died, Mary ran a brothel in her big house down in Birmingham, Alabama. But before that she was a maid at a whites-only hotel in downtown Birmingham where she could only come and go through the back door. When my father would send me and my sister down in the summers of our childhood, I would wince at the Colored and Whites Only bathrooms and water fountains that distinguished the South from America's North. The racism, so deeply embedded and pronounced, made the invisible slights I was used to by some teachers and white kids in school seem almost innocuous. I would forgive and forget them every year after summering with my older sister, Aileen.

Mary went by different variations of the same name by different people in our family. My father called his mother *Ma*ma, just like all Southern boys did, but the rest of us pronounced it with equal stress on both syllables (as in *Mah-Mah*), so that's what my mother and we grandkids called her. My son and her other great-grandchildren called her Big Mama. And unlike his grandmother—*my* mother—my son often marveled that, as he put it, "Big Mama is not a sweet old lady."

She had never been sweet. Solidly built and broad-featured, she was, as she can say now, "Never been no pretty woman. But I could dress."

137

And that was true. Mama was not a pretty woman but she carried herself like one. Born to the children of slaves, you would have thought this matriarch was a monarch the way she walked in to church in her ornamental hats, starched dresses, and wavy bouffant wig. The only woman that I can think of who reminds me of her personal style and carriage is Queen Elizabeth II. She was not a pretty woman either but she could dress.

Thankfully, for the sake of my family's genetic prospects, she married a beautiful man. My grandfather was a no-good handful of a husband and a deadbeat father but he was as pretty as a man can be. Tall, lean, and caramel skinned, with fine-features, a square-jaw, and with what the old folks used to call good hair, he had what I guess you could call leading-man looks today. And he was a ladies man and a drinker, but who could stand in the way of such a good looking man? Not Mama. When she lost her virginity to him at 18 years-old and became pregnant with my father, Papa did what men did back then and married her. But she wasn't what his colorist line of educated, paper-bag-colored, Talented Tenth kinfolk wanted for him so they didn't treat her right. A sharecropper's daughter, the granddaughter of slaves, Mama was thick, big-boned, nappy-headed, full-mouthed, and with a nose nearly as wide as the breadth of her face. She loved my Papa, although she nearly killed him shooting at him twice. Let's just say the majority of her descendants are better looking people for it, if not always better people.

Although married, Mama was practically a single mother for a large part of my father's upbringing. Papa didn't come home sometimes for days or weeks and other women in the neighborhood had his babies out of wedlock so often that Mama's humiliation became as embedded and yet inscrutable as her own genes. She knew the women because she could see her husband in their babies. And yet she could walk on by with her head held high because at least she had married the man. That other woman just borrowed him. And now she had a child to feed all by herself.

I decided to gift my grandmother a trip down South for her 99th birthday. We were to stay as guests at the very hotel she used to clean, long-since integrated, it was to be a surprise. She thought we would be staying with her less refined and countrified, and only-living sister,

Annabelle. She thought that only I would be staying in a hotel while she and her sister could reconnect in their later years, possibly for the last time.

I had booked the trip for my entire off-days, Saturday through Tuesday, packed for both of us, and was looking forward to that dense Alabama heat I remember from my youth visits, the kind that just makes you feel it in your bones that this was the climate and atmosphere your kind of folks were meant to live in. In the cold winters up north, there is the primordial sense of being an imposter. This was the weather for the Caucasian, not the Negro. Not the Negress, especially. Anemic like my grandmother, the cold could shoot through me so brutally sometimes in these dark winters that I could weep from the pain just walking to my car in a parking lot leaving the market or department store. And even though it was summer here on her birthday, I still couldn't wait to go down South. The heat there was different. Fuller, more immersive. The heat was in the people and the food and the way you moved in the atmosphere. The South is a different place than the North.

"Mama, you ready?" I called out after I heard her come out of the bathroom the morning of our trip. I had suspected she was already dressed and ready for hours, probably didn't even sleep. At her age, traveling wasn't something she often did. Barely able to climb the four stairs of my split-level home to get to her bedroom, a plane ride was an event for Mama. Like people in the South are wont to do, sometimes her folks—and mine too, I guess—would drive up here with one of her sisters without so much as a warning, let alone an invitation, and stay for days to see her, knowing it might be the last time she and one of her five sisters would ever be together again.

"What, Tresa?" She called back, using her distinctly abbreviated version of my name, Theresa. I had forgotten that lately I have to yell when I talk to her from another room.

"You ready to go, Tresa?" I could hear the excitement in her trembling voice, once so distinctly stentorian and level. My eyes watered a little bit when I thought that she sounded a little bit like an excited child. "Almost time to go," she added.

I knew we had plenty of time, but I didn't want her to worry about missing the flight. My biggest weakness is timeliness so I made sure

I had everything ready the night before and all I had to do was brush my teeth, wash my face, and put our bags in the car. It takes almost 10 minutes just to get her into the car because she moves so slowly and it's a delicate maneuver getting her still heavy, stolid frame into my truck, which requires her to step up and then scoot in. Which is of course easier than when I had my Porsche. I could get her in there but I had to almost dig her out. It didn't help that, unlike my grandmother, I am petite and lean, "po'" as they used to call it down South, so if I pulled my back out helping her in or out we would both be on the ground.

"You take after your mama's peoples," she would remind me often. Sometimes it was just the truth, I didn't look like my grandmother because I did take after my mother's side. What little of me that did look like her arm of my family tree resembled Mama's much more attractive younger sister, Carrie. On the other hand, Aileen looked like Mama, just prettier. And I was pretty too, but lighter-skinned, finer-boned, and petite. So sometimes I wondered when she reminded me that I didn't take after her if it was a reprimand. I probably look to her like the kind of girl her husband's family wanted him to marry. That's probably why she was always nicer to bigger-boned and darker-skinned Aileen than me and Carolyn, our younger sister who was high-yellow with features so fine and a behind so flat she looked practically half-Indian. Carolyn used to joke that if Momma and Daddy had had any more children they would have been white. "By the time they got to me, there was practically nothing left," she would deadpan with a disappointment colored by amusement. Of the four of us—we have an older brother, Clayton—Carolyn most looked, sounded, and even acted like a white woman, and there was always a sense of disingenuousness to her lament about the genes she pretended to be stuck with, even if most of the time she carried herself with so much superiority and aloofness that, while we were growing up, she often seemed more like a visitor than a real member of our family.

Between my pretty grandfather, Mama's deeply West African features, and our mother's mysterious, almost Dickens-like upbringing, Indian blood-mixing, and almost apparition of a father, the range of features between the four of us was so wide that none of us looked, sounded, or even acted related. Our tall, athletic brother was probably the only obvious mix of our two parents, inheriting in equal measure the best and worst looks and personality traits of both branches.

"The service turned Clayton to drinking," Mama would say after one of my brother's annual self-humilations. "And your mama and daddy was soft on him." It was as if the fact that our grandfather was himself also a drunk never made a mental connection. But women in her time made excuses for the men and the boys. But we girls couldn't so much as sit down without our legs crossed or smile at a boy at church without being called fast-tailed and find ourselves quarantined inside the house for an entire adolescent summer.

When I finished dressing, I walked into her room, surprised to find her sitting in the dark, the glow of the television morning show barely outlining her silhouette, fully dressed and be-wigged, a white envelope on her lap. I turned the light on. Before I could ask, she said, "I need you to put this somewhere," and she gave me the envelope. "In your purse. I don't want to lose it."

"Okay, Mama, " I said, taking the envelope without asking what was in it. It felt like cash. Probably hundreds or even thousands of dollars in cash. I put it in my purse, respecting her privacy as an adult. "Let's get you in the car."

"Where my bags?" Her voice quivered.

"In the car already." I smiled and kissed her on the cheek. I knew that she was excited and nervous and, possibly, even skeptical. This was her last trip home. And I knew she knew it.

§

Mama seemed both awed and apprehensive by the expansiveness and modernity of the airport, with all its crowds and broadcast announcements. The last time she had actually been to an airport since she moved up North was almost a decade ago, after my mother died.

"Mama, do you remember the last time you were on an airplane?" I asked her softly, but not quietly. I didn't want to startle her out of her trance.

She paused and stammered. "Well, your daddy died in '83. I came up here. Then I went back home."

I didn't want to correct her. Memory is selective enough even before old age. If it were easier for her to reach back to the Great Depression or cleaning white people's hotel rooms in the 1920s and 30s than remembering being on a plane to move here only eight years ago when my mother passed then that was that. Every person's memory is their own. What is kept and what is repressed or erased is theirs to keep or lose, even if it isn't a choice. My son, for example, has convinced himself that I was both overprotective and emotionally unavailable. And as much as he tries to convince me to reckon with these sins, I just remember always being his mother and loving him from a vantage point entirely out of his depth. I guess memory isn't at all the things that once happened, it's the perspective of them.

"Where my envelope?" she asked before we approached the boarding gate. "I got it," I said. I turned and she looked skeptical, so I opened my purse and let her peek inside to see it.

"What bag is that? That Channel?"

I smiled. "Em hmm, Mama. Chanel."

Well, I got some things from my grandmother. My mother wouldn't know a designer label from a Roman numeral but Mama and I were the clotheshorses in the family. Her asking me what I was wearing or carrying was the closest I would ever get to being genuinely complimented on it.

Walking Mama through the airport toward the gate, I wondered if I had been thoughtless not to ask if she wanted a wheelchair. Our departure gate was a good distance of a walk and with her arm ringed in mine it would take us at least 15 minutes to get there.

"Mama, do you want to get a chair?"

"I ain't need no chair. Once you sit in one them things you don't ever get back up and walk again."

I couldn't argue with the superstition of a nearly 100 year-old black woman. We walked in silence for some time before she said, "I didn't know Detroit had this many white folks." By this point the absurdity of what I was about to get myself into kicked in and I laughed harder than I had in what felt like years. *What on earth was I doing? And what are we going to be doing for four days? Was this even a good idea?*

"I love you, Mama."

A beat. "Love you too, Tresa."

The flight was smooth. I slept through most of it and Mama was uncharacteristically quiet again. She was nervous, I could tell. Nervous about seeing Annabelle? I wondered. Then again, she was probably more nervous about the people she would *not* see. The people who are no longer living and who for most of her life amounted to everyone she knew and everything she knew in Birmingham, Alabama. Where was I taking her? To a place where nothing and almost no one was left? Now I was starting to get the jitters. Suddenly, I wondered about my own life, should David precede me and I not marry again. That would be the end of my line. There would be my sisters and my brother, if they lived. And Clay and Carolyn's children. Aileen didn't have any. I only have one—and he will likely not give me any grandchildren. As disruptive as it must seem to have outlived both her only son and daughter-in-law, making her grandchildren her nearest relatives, it occurred to me when I woke up as we were descending that that's a lot more than I can expect. *Who will be holding my arm through the airport if I lived another 48 years?* The pilot announced that the weather in Birmingham was clear and sunny now but rainfall was expected in the early evening. It was already close to four p.m. now. As we descended, the flight experienced the only turbulence of the trip and for a moment I turned and looked and Mama looked frightened.

"It's just turbulence," I said, putting my hand over hers, which was clutched on the arm rest.

She shook her head in either agreement or faith or maybe neither, as oftentimes her head would tremble for no reason at all, something I started noticing about a year ago. Ataxia, the nurse had called it. After the nurse had left, Mama warned me in what sounded like jest, "Once you get through hot flashes it's gon' be something else every year." Every time I think about that I feel a psychosomatic rush heating up my face that sends the rest of my body chills.

I rented a car but I also knew that this would be the least relaxing part of the trip because I didn't know my way around this city and people drive differently in different places. But I couldn't see myself trapped in a hotel or in my great-aunt Annabelle's dining room for four days and, well, I'm a single woman who is still pretty and who knows what I may feel like doing while Mama is with her—our—family. Shop. Dine. *Husband shop? Prospective husband dine?* I made myself laugh.

"Mom, your life would be so much easier if you were open to dating outside the realm of black men," David had so often said. *Outside the realm of black men*, as only he would put it. *Who talks like that?* David talks like that. Like the white boys he dates . . .

Thinking of my son's interracial sex life was the edge of a perversity I did not want to explore any further so I concentrated on my map while Mama and I waited to deboard. We were in Economy and even though we were close to the first class I knew it was smarter to let everyone get off so we could take our time getting out. But then, isn't there something about the best made plans?

"Tresa," her voice suddenly urgent and demanding, the voice I thought we had left at home. "Tresa, Mama got to get up and pee." I could tell this was not negotiable. "Mama, we can't get up right now. Can you wait?"

The head trembling, her bouffant wig curls quivering. I knew this was not the way we could start this trip. Without asking, I took off my seatbelt and then hers and got her up. Sensing the situation, a very astute and sturdily built male flight attendant, Latino, probably a gay man, appeared. He started, "She has to . . . ?"

"Yes," I whispered with what came out with a tinge of terror. He looked around. "Okay," and then he grabbed her and seemed to whisk Mama off to the lavatory in one swoop. I sighed. I didn't know how many get out of jail cards I had on this trip but one was certainly used before we even touched the ground.

He gently walked her back and buckled her in several minutes later. I even noticed another attendant look at us with a scrutiny that was either empathetic or judgemental, somehow I couldn't tell.

"What's your name?" I said.

He smiled. "Angel."

I laughed. "You can say that again. I hope you don't get in trouble."

"Tsk, I stay in trouble," he said, rolled his eyes with a playful exaggeration, and waved his wrist downward, all in a way that confirmed my suspicion. It was an effeminate gesture that my David would never make. The kind of way about a man that wouldn't make me question if he was really gay after all so much.

"Let me have my envelope," Mama ordered.

"Mama, we can't tip them," I whispered.

"You hear me!"

"Mama, he can't take any money."

"Thank you, Miss Mary, but I'm not allowed," said Angel with a big but nervous smile, and then he darted back to his station as quickly as possible. I knew Mama had been grateful if she had been friendly enough to tell him her name.

"You disavow me . . ." Mama looked at me with a stern coldness—the grandmother of my childhood, my grandmother at 50, my age. There she was again. Except her wig curls quivered in a way that belied the steadiness of her disapproving gaze.

"Mama, the man can't take money. He would get fired." Unfortunately I had to say it loud and firmly because of the engines.

"He can't take no money?"

I wanted so badly to just let it go. But I knew that in order for this trip to work I would have to reassert my dominance. When she made me feel 8 years-old, I would have to remind her that I was the one who was 50 now, not her.

"I'm not gon' let you worry me, Mama." And it worked. I could actually feel her transport back to being sweet and helpless without even turning to look at her. This would be a trip of shape-shifting, I could see.

§

When offered a wheelchair for my grandmother by another flight attendant after we deboarded, I didn't even give her the option. Too early to be this exasperated, I gave in to pragmatism. An hour walking her from the gate to wherever the car rental office was was an hour we didn't have. I was getting hungry and there was supposed to be a change in the weather. I wanted to get the car, get her to the hotel for her surprise, take her to dinner, and go to bed. I knew she would be tired and not expect to see her sister until tomorrow. All I wanted was to get to the hotel, see the look on her face when she recognizes where we are and realizes she can enjoy all the perks of being the guest and not the maid. I felt a surge of boastful self-satisfaction for thinking of such a perfect way to celebrate my grandmother's birthday. I pushed her with a carefully paced briskness through the long and myriad passages of the Birmingham-Shuttlesworth International Airport and she rode without complaint, probably marveling at all of the white folks that are still in Alabama, or who knows what. All I knew was that once I got to that hotel room and in that bed, I was home free.

I had requested a four-door sedan that could easily fit two large women in their 90s in the backseat and I was pleased to see how easily the attendant guided my grandmother into the passenger seat. This was the South, after all, and hospitality and manners came without perk. I did tip this young man and when I got in the car, Mama, never missing a thing, said, "I hope he don't get fired." At this point, I grabbed hold of the steering wheel at ten and two and laughed yet again louder than I have in probably years. It was a mad, bottomless laugh, a surrendering to an impossible comedy of either manners or madness that I had just willfully dived into. *This was going to be National Lampoon's Vacation with My Grandmother. May my ancestors protect us both!*

"You done drank something on that plane?" she asked me.

"Mama. Now, you know I am the only person in this family besides my mother and father, rest their souls, who does not need something to get through something." "Well, you acting like you done had you something ... maybe it's that high air."

Lord Jesus! What have I gotten myself into! When I could finally stop laughing, I took a deep breath and Mama said, "You know how to drive a car like this, here? You know it's hillier down in here."

"Mama, I am a *Detroit* girl. I can drive *anything*." I drove us out of the airport, windows down, the hot air gushing in my face.

"We're home, Mama!" I announced with more cheer than even I expected. I looked over at her. I could not tell if she was nodding her head up and down in agreement or if this was the head trembling again.

146

"Is that too much air?" I pressed the button for her window to go up some on her side. "Put that back down," she said.

§

On our way out of the airport campus my cell phone rang. I took a quick glance at the number and saw from the first three digits that it was Aileen, calling to make sure that we landed safely, no doubt. Aileen smoked weed, used to smoke coke, still smokes cigarettes, was married to a man who threatened to kill her and that she threatened to kill on numerous occasions, and lived in a neighborhood in the house we grew up in where these days bullets are known to fly into the windows of random residences, but her mortal fear was flying. I knew I better pull over.

"We landed, I was going to call you when we got to the hotel," I said. "Mama, say hi to Aileen," I said a few octaves higher, putting Aileen on speakerphone, which I should have told her.

"You got the car?"

"We are in it now."

"Okay, well call me when you get settled in. And try not to kill our grandmother." Snicker. "Aileen! You're on speaker—"

"On what?" Puff. "Well, what you think, I'm supposed to see you through the damn phone? You da one could have said something!"

"Girl, bye! Love you!" I turned off the speakerphone. "And can you call David to let him know we landed?."

"Roger that. Love you too." And then an octave louder, "Love you, Mama!" but I was sure Mama could not discern any of this with her hearing and, now as she was, back in her trance state. She was home now and whatever she was hearing at this moment probably happened before I was even born.

Birmingham, Alabama, is a city of hills and mountains and red dirt and a mini-metropolis of modest skyscrapers giving way to the legacies of prosperous antebellum grandeur and barefoot rural despair in equal measure. The air smelled differently, the food more savory, the mosquito bites larger and itchier. Everything here had more sugar, more salt, more heat, more fragrance. The South's renown civility

147

and expressive politeness belied its notorious ruthlessness. I thought about my father and how quickly and decisively he chose to take my mother and their newborn son as far away from here as possible when he returned from Italy after the war. So many millions like him did. Like Mama, both of my parents had a pantheon of stories about Southern life from that time and of the stories dared to be told, I could only wonder about the ones that were too unmentionable. There may not have been any more strange fruit hanging but nobody ever cut down those trees. They were still here.

A white family in a large pickup truck—a half dozen kids in the cab—laughed and screeched and swore in a jovial, boisterous way, had pulled up next to me at the light on the way out of the airport's last thoroughfare. Loud as they were, I realized I couldn't understand them. Then I remembered that twang, the way white folks down South *sang* when they spoke. And my people, some of us seemed to mumble almost incomprehensibly. A cousin of ours who came up for my father's funeral whom I hadn't seen since my grandfather's funeral—Julia would be her name—had a way of speaking that was so dense and regional that then ten year-old David had tugged on my black skirt and asked, "Is she deaf?" It was a moment that was almost funny, but for my recognition that, while I could at least comprehend her version of English, a thread was broken by my son and the upper-middle class upbringing I was giving him. The way his people spoke for hundreds of years by way of necessity and survival was in one generation falling on deaf ears.

This would be a weekend of things remembered, I braced myself, and of things deliberately forgotten.

Finally outside of the BHM campus, I turned onto the I-59 and the sky did that thing that it does when the weather system doesn't give you a warning that things are about to change. The sky had been nearly cloudless just minutes ago, the sun shining from a seemingly originless perspective, and now a bolt of lightning suddenly sizzled overhead. I had forgotten about Southern storms and how urgent and theatrical they could be. I knew then that I wanted to get downtown as soon as possible because I didn't know these roads as it was and a storm would make a riddle out of my already shaky sense of direction.

"You gon' take the I-59 West to Avaughn Road, now." Mama seemed to be confident that she remembered her city.

"I think we have to take this to Exit 138," I said.

"The what? You go to Avaughn Road."

"Well, we are going to my hotel first."

"We go downtown now?"

"Yes."

"Take this to Avaughn Road."

"Mama, let me take care of the driving, you just relax and look at these beautiful mountains—"

"Look like the Lord about to come out the sky 'bout now," she said. "I hope I didn't come all the way down here just to be caught up in the Rapture."

The sky did change abruptly from clear to ominously overcast and if I weren't starting to get a little nervous I would have laughed.

"Well you would certainly be able to say you had lived to see it all then," I muttered, although not really, since she most certainly couldn't hear me.

We didn't speak for a while and I couldn't find whatever road she was talking about so I willfully forgot about it while I concentrated on stewarding us along the five miles toward downtown the way I remembered from the simple directions I'd taken from someone at the hotel over the phone.

"Your father was born in a storm," she said after a while, staring ahead.

"You gave me that blanket."

"I gave your momma that blanket. Aileen got it now."

"No, Mama. I have it. Everything you have is at my house."

"Carolyn tried to steal it."

"Carolyn did not try to—" I started to chuckle. "We not gon' go backwards, Mama. Carolyn didn't know it was your blanket."

"I don't know whose people she take after."

149

I took a deep breath. "Well. I can't say I do either."

Exit 142 flew by. Ours is 138. As the overcast became more prominent, I decided to turn on the radio so there could be something to take the edge off of both of our anxiety. What had turned into anticipation and excitement was starting to feel a little jittery for some reason. I couldn't put my finger on it.

I pulled into the right lane and exited the ramp for 138. I pressed the button on both of our windows to roll them up to just a peek, as the hot breeze had turned into a chill. As I decelerated toward the light, I realized that my famous intuition was doing its job. Detour signs and construction cones were directing us away from the turn I needed to make and toward a hilly incline on a residential looking street that was going away from downtown and toward Red Mountain, the tall ridges that curved around the city in a way that made Birmingham feel ensconced inside a shell. That tall Vulcan statue that looks over the city like the *Christ the Redeemer* statue in Rio seemed to beckon us toward it in a way that didn't seem far removed from Mama's Rapture reference.

"You know where you goin—"

"Mama!" I didn't mean to raise my voice quite that way. "Let me get my bearings." I rounded the corner and when the construction worker waving the traffic flag was close enough to hear me, I rolled down my window and shouted, "How do I get back to downtown?" The dark pink-skinned white man looked at me with a snarl and kept waving me toward the opposite direction I wanted to go. I repeated my question.

"Get!" He shouted. "Go'on!"

Wow. So that happened. I could only keep following traffic and assume that all of these people are being detoured from their route too and that most of them know where they are going. So until I could figure out a moment to stop and pull over I just followed the traffic. "Going up Red Mountain," Mama muttered, shaking her head.

And that's when the first roll of thunder cried.

"Gotta be a damn gas station over here *somewhere*," I said to no one. Then again, did I really want more of what I just got? I would have to wait to find some black folks. But the further I drove the less commercial or even residential the landscape became until finally we were on a two-way road that curved like a trail through the Red Mountain region that overlooks the city. As the mountain walls encroached the city grew darker and then blip . . . blip . . . blip, the raindrops hit my windshield in globs so thick I could barely discern the yellow line in the middle of the road. And there was no place to pull over. All I could do at this point was just drive. The road's slickness made me trepid about the pressure I put on the gas pedal in this unfamiliar car so I braked and gassed, braked and gassed. The person behind me must have been doing the same because they weren't riding me. I followed the orange tail lights in front of me, avoided the white headlights to the left of me, and slowed down when I saw red brake lights in front of me, but that was essentially all I could see. The traffic slowed. The raindrops gave way to a steady stream of precipitation until another roll of thunder and streak of lightning illuminated this cave-like valley until everything was momentarily white. A cascade of water seemed to gush onto the windshield and as horns honked and more thunder growled, I fixed my eyes on the tail lights in front of me as they went from white to red to white to red again and at one point my distance perception was so distorted that I almost hit them. My heart rate increased and the uncertainty in Mama's silence invited a thought I didn't want: that I was frightened. *What had I done?* This was a terrible idea, all of it. I had made a mistake and now I—we—are in danger.

Ain't no way. Like the gospel song. Ain't no way this is going to be our way out of here. Jesus has taken me too far, both of us too far, to let me down now. I told myself, *I don't know where I am or how I got here but I have been here before. And He will shepherd me. Lord Jesus . . .*

Multiple thunder crackled and roared into all out booms, sometimes rolling into and over one another like two Sopranos in a duet. A power struggle between two like essences from different sources is not a symbiosis but a competition. Like me and Mama. We had learned to live and fight and put out fires and all without a man. Or, sometimes the man was the fight, the fire. Was that what we needed now? The visual spatial authority and confidence of a *man* driving us through this storm? Was there a limit to how much a woman could do? Had I used all of my get-of-woman jail cards?

The windshield wipers swayed unsteadily along the glass in front of me and I wondered if I were one torn inch of plastic away from careening into the side of a mountain or another car. Brake, gas, brake, gas, and then it happened. The sound of metal hitting metal in a way no other event makes and, though while I knew it wasn't us, it was someone, somewhere near us. Sirens commenced seemingly immediately from no particular direction, and as another roll of thunder growled, the mezzo Soprano, I just said it, I said, as loudly as I could, "Lord Jesus, see us through!" And I screamed. I screamed. I put the hazards on and I stopped the car and I just screamed and cried and I shouted and I just called His name. I felt Mama's hand clutch my wrist and I just gripped the steering wheel, my sobs as unstoppable as the rain, and Mama just said, "I got you, baby. You all right. God got us. God got us, baby. We gon' get through. We gon' get through this storm, baby."

And I cried and it rained and I screamed and I prayed and it thundered back like a call-and-response oratory so timed I felt the thunder and lightning reinforcing and punctuating for my deliverance, as opposed to a weapon formed against me. I shouted His name and He clapped back. The sky lit. The atmosphere grunted and moaned. And when I was out of tears so there it was. The clapping. I almost didn't see him. That wasn't thunder. That was a young police officer knocking on my window. I pressed the button that rolled it down.

"Do you need assistance?" the young white officer said.

"I'm lost. I'm trying to . . ." I realized it was clear I had been sobbing my eyes out. "I need to get my grandmother downtown!" And I burst into tears again.

"Okay, well there's been an accident a few cars up. Why don't you pull over to the edge of the ridge next to my car—actually. I'm going to call you a tow. This is a rental?" "Yes," I blubbered between sobs.

"I'll have it towed. You have a hotel downtown?"

"Yes! Yes. You can take us?"

"Absolutely, Ma'am. Just pull over to the side over there. I'm going to call for backup for this accident and then I'll come out and stop the traffic so you can get in my car." "Jesus! Okay, thank you," I told him, hyperventilating.

"Okay, just go on over there and don't get out of the car until I come for you." "Somebody hit us?" Mama asked.

"No, no, ma'am," he said and then he walked into the stalled traffic. "I'm going to take you and your daughter to—er, your granddaughter to your hotel."

I waited for the car ahead of me to move up a little bit but I didn't feel like I even understood where the officer said his car was parked. There were no side ramps. There was no shoulder. There was no place to pull over. This was just two lanes enclosed between two walls of mountain.

The rain abated almost as suddenly as it started and the sky began to clear a bit. I felt my skin crack along my cheeks where my tears had fallen and dried.

"I'm sorry, Mama," I muttered.

Somehow she heard me. "We gon' make it now, baby. Come too far!" She tapped my thigh.

The traffic moved again and I crept along the still-slick roads looking for the officer or his car. There was no officer and no car. Not for minutes and then not for what was at least a mile before there was a ramp that led to a decline and for all my lack of sense of direction, I just took it down. I may not know north from west but I know up from down and we needed to get *down* off of this mountain.

As we traveled downward I could see the skyline of downtown in the distance, the Vulcan hovering on the other side of us, and the lanes widened and the environment became more residential and then commercial and finally, actually, familiar. I started to recognize some of these hilly roads and if not the actual stores and landmarks, the unnameable essence of a city that speaks to you in a certain familiar language when you haven't been there in a long time. I'm not going to say that the sun came out because it didn't, but it stopped raining. And eventually we were on an overpass driving across the I-59, where we had started, and we were on our way. We were on our way to the Grand LaSalle Hotel.

"Birmingham done spread out," Mama said as her streets rolled by.

"John had a debt over here somewhere I had to pay or them Indians was gon' slit his throat. I had to come over here in my uniform so they didn't kill my husband. Told that redbone Indian man next time just tell me, I'll kill him for you." And she laughed. I wasn't ready to laugh yet but I laughed anyway. "How did you finally stop him from gambling?" I said, suddenly curious.

"I didn't. That multiple sclerosis sure as hell did it for me. *And* the drinking." I chuckled. "That would do it."

"I had to hide my money in so many places in that house I bet there's still some money in them walls. Whoever living there now . . ."

"I loved that house." Mama's house from my childhood had an open-floor plan that used to go around and around in a circle around a big stairwell. Aileen and I would just walk around all day those summers playing *Gone with the Wind*. And if we got in trouble Mama would chase us around that stairwell with a switch or a belt until my Papa, a laid-up invalid at this point with the bawdy sense of humor of the drunk who had tricked life into letting him think he had won, he would laugh and say, "You gon' make 'em hate you, Mary!"

"Where *was* that house? Do you think it's still there?" I said.

Mama turned to me, seemingly startled and affronted by the question. "Avaughn Road," she pronounced.

§

The Grand LaSalle Hotel was built in 1891, as the engraving near the entrance attests, and was once a pillar of downtown Birmingham's economy and society. For at least two decades it was the only luxurious hotel in the city and then by the Roaring 20s it was said to maintain its perch over the competition by cleverly hosting Prohibition speakeasy parties for the high-rollers in town. What in other circumstances might have diminished its allure actually saved it from succumbing to the Great Depression. This is the period when my grandmother, Mary E. Stubbs, worked there with the other colored girls who cleaned the rooms (it was all they hired for that, she told me) of an establishment that would not accept black people as guests for another 30 years and until then only allowed black workers like my grandmother to enter and exit through the back door, which was still another back door than the one the white employees used.

By now, though, the hotel had seen better days and it was owned by a corporate chain that (almost) discreetly called it the *Wyatt* Grand LaSalle. But it's facade still bore the impression of stuffy, imperious, and ostentatious luxury that would impress a woman of my grandmother's age far more than the understated boutique hotels whose luxuriousness manifested itself with minimalism and glass as opposed to columns, ornamental moldings, and *bas relief.*

When I stopped in front of the valet on the side of the hotel, I wasn't sure if it registered with Mama that we were here. And who knows, maybe she wouldn't even be as impressed as I had hoped. I certainly wasn't. But after the attendant helped her out of the car and we followed as he took our bags toward the portico steps before the front doors, my grandmother, arm ringed through mine, stopped so abruptly that I almost tripped.

"Mama?"

This was the moment I was waiting for. We were stopped in front of the entrance of the Grand LaSalle, its half dozen steps leading to heavy, faux oak doors, the columns and lions and monarchs looming over the doorway in all of their almost camp glory.

"We're here." I said. "This is where we're staying."

Mama didn't say anything. Instead, she took her arm out of mine and walked toward the banisters. One of the valets who flanked the front doors walked down the portico toward her and gingerly escorted her up the steps. The other appeared to come for me, assuming that the reason I was still standing before the stairs was because I was a woman in need of chivalry to lead me up the stairs of this fadingly glorious hotel. I shook my head and smiled, declining his assistance. Then I slowly watched my grandmother, Mary E. Stubbs, carry herself like a queen through the entry hall of the Grand LaSalle which was, gratefully, far more authentically luxuriously renovated on the inside than I was expecting. This was more my style. I walked to the reception desk to check in. Looking around, I realized that about two-thirds of the guests were black. Middle-class families and well-to-do *bourgies* sauntered around casually and semi-formally against a din of Southern respectability and almost regality. I didn't see Mama for a second but then I felt her and suddenly there she was, walking like the queen she's always been.

"You know where we are, Mama?"

Her head trembled and she lowered it, trying to control the ataxia. But she was too excited and her head and that wig just quivered and shook until she surrendered to her quiet achievement. "Let me have that envelope."

For a second I'd forgotten about that.

"Miss Theresa, your room keys," the man behind the desk smiled with teeth so perfect he looked like a dental model.

"Thank you," I said, taking the keys. I opened my purse and took the envelope out and gave it to Mama. "Where is the elevator?" I asked the man.

"Just around the way to the right of the grand staircase," he said.

"Come on, Mama," I said, holding out my elbow for her to take my arm.

"Hold on, now," she warned. Gingerly, she opened the envelope and took out one long white glove and slipped it down her arm. And then another on the other arm. She then put her arm through mine and we walked toward the elevator.

"Tomorrow we gon' get you some gloves," she said, her head nodding, but deliberately now.

Untitled

by Nina Hook

Make sure to color in the lines with a sharpened orange colored pencil; I'll press the ends of the empanadas if you make the filling; wash the dishes with stinging hot water from the well; pretend to glance away when he locks eyes with you; lace your shoes with two bunny ears like Miss Beth taught you; go into the country club across the pond, but make sure your shoulders aren't showing—temptation! I'll teach you those Spanish curse words so you can slash others with your tongue without repercussion; find a ring by spring; make sure you only do drugs and drink behind the veil; if the veil is torn, expect exclusion; swim in Colorado river and jump off the rope—splash! break your bones fitting in the Southwest mold; love Sunday service and children's gospel songs; praise the sunset and curse the devil; ride the sand dunes above the mountain to the coast; don't come back, all you need is to remember home; sip the tortilla soup and spiced tea laced with gossip and Jesus; pretend you know why, but never ask questions; apply sunscreen at least twice a day; arrive at the airport one hour early (even though it is 5 mins away and only has one gate); cry as the engine of the airplane roars, but only because you are scared, not because you will tiptoe back; if you do come back, it best be with blood dripping from your nose to curse the sky with those Spanish words I taught you.

The Southwest Storm: A Collection of Mini Stories

by Nina Hook

I am no architect. I can barely draw a shaky stick figure on the back of faded receipts. I am no architect, but I can build. I can build sentences like a canyon's wall emerges from Earth's core, giving solace in the depths. I learned a groveling, knees-in-dirt type of building from my grandfather. My grandfather, my architect, had a keen eye for structure, how to draw a blueprint for three unexpected children, how to make the kitchen big enough to fit a jukebox and 50s diner, how to create the A-frame yellow house, looking out towards the looming border of Mexico. How to build between the lines of cultures and engulf them both. He built this A-frame from the ground up, and it became a sanctuary in the small town of Gadsden, Arizona. It stood proud on Highway 95, the sun spreading its golden frosting on each piece of wood. Each nerve in your body would tell you you're safe, you're home, as you walked along the white, lacy flower beds to the red front door. In the living room, you would look up to the sky to see the tip of the home coming together, pointing to the stars that my grandfather would catch each night as he rested on the back patio. Dust and the desert moon were his closest friends before the rooster crowed at dawn.

My grandmother was the keeper of each and every cranny tucked with a historic realm or sentimental piece from seasons of her life, worn yet vibrant like a faded polaroid. I could feel her skinny, soft and worn hands wrap around each antique in the living room, how each roll of the empanada dough was maintained, how the morning parakeet greeted her with ecstatic sounds, how each weak cup of coffee was laced with something far greater, how each and every room in the house held old relics that she would talk about with pride, how her greatest pride was her grandchildren, their photos hung on every open space. I can still see six-year-old me looking at the lens with my cowboy hat and red lips, knowing my home was snuggled in between the side of the glass cabinet where the keeper sticks picture after picture of her grandchildren. That little girl had the privilege of watching my grandma make tacos, rice, and beans every day—the smells wafering around the kitchen like a steam bath, cleaning her senses and forming a palate of nostalgia.

The keeper was tidy and clean; she would make dear friends with the rooster and crow at the earliest sign of sun. Her power vacuum would always sound louder than their voices. She knew she won the competition. She felt control in her A-frame house the architect had purposefully built for her. It was her desert thunderstorm where she could manage the destruction of its wind. The keeper would stay up late, too. As the sun went down, the control was undone with each button pressed on the jukebox. She was free to release all that was kept in a day's worth of work. Her hips would sway to the grainy tones of 50s classics. She would spin and jump and let her wind pick up. Her denim shorts wrinkling with each movement, bending to the sound of the beat. Keeping was not a job for the faint of heart. It required a lot to be bottled up. Yet, when the music was flowing into her ears, down her back, through her veins, she wasn't the keeper anymore. She was the desert dust devil, and the black and white tiled floor felt like hopscotch. Her childlike spirit was kept with the wild west wind. She was spinning free.

§

It was 1964, and the sparkles from the 1962 Pontiac, just cleaned and glittering in the Arizona sun, made Dee's eyes catch, almost as much as the cowboy in it. Dee could barely see as the mixing of the sun and heat and dust created a dust devil whirring up inside her, but she knew already what she wanted. Louie walked out with little notice of Dee or her goo-goo-eyed friends on the bleachers. He grabbed his baseball bag, locked his car, and went out to the field, shaking his teammates' hands as he walked up. The air laid on her skin in tiny droplets that felt like the freedom of summer. The dry heat raised young high school cravings of vanilla *con leche raspados*, Big League bubblegum, and sex. Dee wanted far more. Louie, tanned skin and nasty armed, warmed up his pitching game. *The Yuma Daily Sun* reported he was going places. The Arizona Diamondbacks, even. In every game the stats would come in, showing he was destined for the major leagues (he was only missing the chewing tobacco vice). Dee strutted confidently in denim shorts and a tank with some white sneakers, showing off her tiny bod (she was under 5 feet tall). Just enough skin showing not to be at the mercy of the vacuum cord from her mom when she tip-toed home. As she watched Louie play ball, she slid onto the top of his sparkling car, just washed. A diamond in the rough of the desert, she sat patiently. Dee hollered at the right plays and whistled toward only one, the sun and dirt and sweat making a melting potion of deliriousness that would last their lifetime. Louie won the game with his major league pitching, but did not realize the heat settling, tension as thick as a cowboy standoff in a saloon. As he came out of the field, sweaty and glistening, he saw Dee sitting on the top of his newly washed car. His forehead wrinkled and he breathed deep with annoyance,

"Get off my car, please."

"No."

"*Vamos*. I don't like anyone sittin' on the hood of my car."

"Well, I don't have to go anywhere because you're gonna marry me, someday."

The Yuma Daily Sun was almost right, Louie made it about as far as he could get. The Diamondbacks were dangling from his lips like a dog dripping from thirst on a hot desert day. But he injured his shoulder, and the dust devil spun the cowboy into staying.

Dee was spot on, though. Less than a year later, they were taking vows in a courtroom, tying the lasso to one another. The dust devil and cowboy are still dancing in the saloon with the sweat and sun, nearly 60 years later.

§

The keeper may not have needed saving, but she needed support, which many people often forgot. She had fought and thrashed and kept her life neatly packaged together despite the blows that hit. She was a survivor, a keeper of precious memories and love, but also of the pain she would never outrun. Through the years, the small town in Arizona found the keeper to be a solace, a beauty, a timeless wonder. Yet, even still, racism ran through the town like a crater, like the earthquake on Easter that emptied the country club pools and ran its hands clumsily through the rich fields of lettuce.

The keeper had driven into the bigger town of Yuma to grab some groceries and supplies for the farm, parking her little car into a wide space in the lot. As she got out, a truck rammed into the back of her car. Astonished, yet calm, she went up to talk to the folks, get their insurance and sort the whole thing out. The damage wasn't too bad, just a small dent. As the keeper walked up, ready to fix and maintain, the strings were pulled loose by the American ideal of purity, whiteness, and a whole lot of fucking bullshit.

An older white woman got out of the car, screaming slurs at my grandmother, telling her to go back where she came from, that she was a disgrace to America. My grandmother gently pleaded for the insurance, not wanting any trouble, the keeper in her taking precedence. Her winds were only a breeze because she knew the danger of a storm with white folks of the town. She would never win. The woman would not back down and called her older son to join. Soon, my grandmother, the keeper of culture, love, and passion, was surrounded with threats and degrading words. The keeper ran to her truck and left, not caring any longer about the insurance. The real damage was already done.

She called my mother, sobs the only thing either of us could hear over the speaker phone. Not one word came out clear until she calmed down. My mom consoled my grandmother and wrapped warm, comforting words around her. I felt tears on my cheeks for all the things I felt would never change; how much my grandmother fought for her life and freedom; how hard she had worked; how much she threw her fists and kept her family, her pain neatly together; how it could all be unraveled because she was not white. I felt this pain in my chest, to not be able to protect her, that I would never understand the hardships she and my mother went through. I would never understand because my skin was white, my last name was white, and my privilege centered on whiteness, despite my Mexican heritage. There was a gulf that stood between us, and I felt it swallow us all.

It was this day, where the keeper was worn and broken and snot ran down her shirt, that I realized she needed someone to be the keeper for her, too. Life felt too much like the Grand Canyon chasm to be dealt with alone.

If the role of the keeper is passed down each generation, I will gladly take it, wrapping the wind around my pointer finger, just like my grandmother does—even on the days where I can only muster a breeze.

§

My grandmother, Delia, has the skinniest, softest worn hands, and mine are skinny and soft and worn, too. Her hands work as a mother, a wife, a storyteller. I find my labor in the art of the creative: words and pictures. We are one and the same, a generational line passed down as keepers of something far greater than any empanada or metaphorical paragraph could express. For my grandmother, it was clear she yearned for control, as my mother does, and as I do, yet her freedom flew like the changing of formation in the sand dunes. She could not be bottled up. She was a force. She could only be caught when she had finished the race, tracing her *rastro de estrellas* with a pointed finger and a hearty laugh.

One late night, my grandmother had topped my coffee and squeezed my hand, soft as the butter she used every morning for the toast and warm as the pumpkin empanadas she always made just for me. Everyone else knew her as a desert force, blowing the sand dunes any way she wished, but with me, she was a soft summer thunderstorm. She told me tale after tale, myth and truth lodged in between the checkered tiles and red-painted bricks. We reminisced on her post-back surgery craze where she would get on the roof of the house to blow off the leaves (just in spite of the doctors and loved ones telling her to take it easy); the pain she felt when her father left her and created a new family just over state lines into the lushing gold rush of California; the love she had for her adopted sister, a protectiveness laced heavy with boldness and courage; and her love for me, playing dress up and helping me pluck peacock feathers that had fallen in the cage, dancing and drinking Coca-Cola till I thought I would throw up.

"Nina, did I ever tell you how your grandpa and I met?"

I smiled, knowingly, "Of course, grandma."

"How about that time this dumbass ran his car into me and flipped me off, so I stopped my car at the red light, went up to his window, and punched him senseless?"

I could hear my grandpa snore, deep in and out, a cowboy lassoing his stars, knowing his best catch was inside making weak coffee and empanadas.

§

On my 21st birthday, amidst cake and homemade Mexican tacos and horchata, my keeper showed me the back of the jukebox. There on a yellow sticky note was my name for when she no longer was around to swirl the wind with her dancing.

murmullo

by Valentina López-Pérez

noche quieta
aire denso
pelo pegado al cuello

me consumo en la profundidad de un recuerdo
que me quema de adentro hacia fuera

el silencio pesa con palabras inconclusas
palabras desmembradas
sonidos errantes

el tic toc del reloj marca la infinidad atolondrada

oscuridad que palpita
oscuridad que gime
oscuridad que cruje

flores marchitas en el alféizar de la ventana

aire que pesa
la cabeza me pesa
cuerpo que pesa sin más

el tic toc del reloj impregna las paredes

eco sin forma

eco sin cuerpo

eco que busca cuerpo en el cuerpo que reposa en la
oscuridad

adentro en el fondo del silencio

yace el retazo de un recuerdo

noche quieta

aire denso

pelo pegado al cuello

consciencia de un cuerpo

y el tic toc del reloj

setakki

by Valentina López-Pérez

saqué los trapitos al sol
y los sequé en el patio de mi casa

la ropa sucia se lava en casa

lavé el pocillo del café
tendí la cama

abrí la ventana para que la casa se aireara

me senté en la butaca
y en silencio esperé

a que mi casa fuera casa

Fuga nº 9

by Luiza Guimarães

1º movimento — Leila

Leila tocava no piano as notas vazias da Nona Sinfonia de Beethoven. Desde que começara seus estudos, aos três anos de idade, as notas de "Ode à Alegria" haviam sido parafusadas em seu cérebro. Ela nunca perguntou o porquê. Era como as coisas deveriam ser. Boas meninas aprendiam a tocar o piano para entreter os futuros convidados das futuras casas as quais comandariam com graça e sem deixar transparecer os esforços.

Olhando o piso de madeira, o sol do fim da tarde entrando pelas janelas e a brisa de verão soprando levemente as cortinas brancas para dentro de casa, Leila não conseguia sentir outra coisa a não ser o fracasso. Onde estava a casa cheia de filhos e netos que lhe tinha sido prometida? Com seu marido amoroso e firme, os empregados e talvez uma ou outra vizinha enxerida?

Naquela sala só havia ela, o piano e os porta-retratos. Fotografias que pareciam zombar da música alegre que Leila insistia em martelar com os dedos no piano, uma mímica perfeita de como havia aprendido cada nota tantos anos atrás.

Os porta-retratos pareciam uma espécie em extinção. Ela já havia visitado os filhos e netos e percebera que a relação idade versus porta-retratos seguia uma progressão geométrica decrescente.

Culpava o celular.

A música e seus pensamentos foram invadidos pelo som da buzina de um carro no portão. Mentalmente, Leila xingou a motorista com palavras que nunca deveriam ser ditas em voz alta por uma senhora respeitável, muito menos direcionadas à própria filha. Mas ela já não havia dito à Carla para tocar a campainha? Custava descer do carro? Cumprimentar a mãe, tomar um café, talvez conversar um pouco?

Leila suspirou, se levantou e foi até a porta, sem se incomodar em fechar o piano ou as janelas. Sentiu-se rebelde e imaginou a mãe repreendendo-a do alto de seu trono no céu, ao lado do Senhor.

Ela abriu a porta e travou uma pequena guerra contra a artrite nos dedos, que tornava muito mais difícil do que o aceitável clicar os minúsculos botões do controle remoto que abria o portão. Sua neta, Isabela, pulou do carro com a mochila da escola.

A menina usava o uniforme puído do colégio. A mochila nas costas era a mesma do ano passado. Leila já havia sondado a filha para saber se passavam alguma necessidade, mas as respostas lhe pareceram muito vagas para que chegasse a uma conclusão. Gostaria de poder perguntar-lhe diretamente, mas não era educado.

O carro novo, recém-emplacado, porém, lhe dizia que talvez a menina só fosse apegada à mochila velha mesmo.

— Vó! — cumprimentou Isabela, com um abraço.

Era uma criança muito carinhosa. Leila gostava dos seus afagos.

— Oi, minha filha! Sua mãe não vai entrar?

— Não. Ela tá com pressa.

Leila acenou para a filha que, dessa vez, ao menos se dignou a abrir a janela para acenar de volta. O carro deu a ré e saiu para a rua assim que o portão fechou.

— Tô com fome, vó! — reclamou a menina.

— Vou preparar um lanche para você. Depois vamos para o piano.

— Tá bom!

Tão linda e obediente. A netinha dos sonhos de qualquer avó. Isabela tinha nove anos e, desde os seis, passava duas tardes por semana estudando piano com a avó. Leila gostava de passar o tempo com a pequena e Carla aproveitava o tempo sem a criança para fazer sabe-se-lá-o-quê as mães fazem sozinhas hoje em dia.

Verdade, a menina era distraída e agitada. Mas os tempos mudaram, graças a Deus, porque se Isabela fosse depender um dia de suas habilidades musicais para conquistar um marido, Leila temia que ela acabasse para titia.

Ainda assim, um pouco de graça e delicadeza não fazem mal a uma menina. Então era vinte minutos de lanche e, depois, os já velhos conhecidos acordes de "Ode à Alegria" pelas próximas horas.

2º movimento — Carla

Por que Beethoven? Por que sempre tem que ser Beethoven?

Enquanto dirigia, Carla esperava na linha do atendimento da companhia telefônica. Havia assinado um plano de internet com o dobro de velocidade para poder trabalhar de casa pela manhã e passar mais tempo com a filha. Só que, desde a assinatura, parecia que o sinal viajava do modem até o seu computador nas costas de uma tartaruga.

Já havia recebido duas advertências no trabalho, pois só conseguiu a liberação do meio período com a garantia de que estaria à disposição em casa. Era simplesmente impossível fazer uma reunião por vídeo-chamada com a conexão atual. E, se para passar mais tempo com a filha, ela precisaria aguentar . . . 40 minutos? Já? Enfim, se precisava aguentar 40 minutos ouvindo a performance de *Für Elise* executada por um robô, que seja! Com sorte conseguiria ser atendida antes de chegar ao mercado.

Carla virou em uma das avenidas congestionadas com o trânsito do final da tarde. As luzes traseiras dos carros brilhavam vermelhas contra suas pupilas e o cheiro de fumaça entrava de algum jeito pelas janelas fechadas. Um reflexo perfeito da sua vida, ela pensou. Presa no meio de vários desconhecidos que também tentavam chegar aos seus compromissos, sufocando lentamente com o escapamento alheio.

Quando percebeu que nem a chamada com a companhia telefônica, nem o trânsito iriam mudar nos próximos minutos, Carla abriu, cuidadosamente, o Instagram. A chamada continuou em espera. Ela começou a rolar, hesitante, o feed e o robô deu seguimento à sua apresentação musical. Ela relaxou e olhou para a tela do aparelho em suas mãos.

Ali estava a irmã, de férias na Disney com os sobrinhos. No próximo post, o irmão, acampando com o marido em algum lugar exótico. A amiga da faculdade, comemorando uma promoção no trabalho. A mãe da Júlia, melhor amiga da filha, compartilhando nas stories uma festinha de aniversário.

Isa não havia sido convidada para essa festinha. Será algum problema na escola? Ou seria a aniversariante apenas uma amiguinha que Júlia conhecia de outro lugar?

Carla precisou relembrar a si mesma, pela décima ou talvez décima primeira vez no dia, que o que via no Instagram não era real. As férias da irmã foram em janeiro. O lugar exótico onde o irmão e o marido estavam era uma das várias trilhas ao redor da cidade que eles sempre fazem todo o fim de semana. Ela mesma já os tinha acompanhado uma vez e quase morrera de tédio. Paravam a cada cinco minutos para tirar uma foto e passavam o resto do percurso reclamando dos mosquitos, da umidade ou das subidas cheias de pedregulhos.

Carla trabalhava com produção de conteúdo para redes sociais. Rolar o feed do seu Instagram pessoal era um ato de estudo ao mesmo tempo que de procrastinação. Mais um dos paradoxos que fazem todo sentido na era digital.

Culpava o celular.

O telefone vibrou em suas mãos com uma chamada em espera. Sua reação imediata foi olhar para o viva-voz do carro, assegurando-se que o robô continuava na sua sinfonia de 55 minutos e 49 segundos. 50. 51. 52.

Alívio. A ligação não tinha caído. Olhou o identificador de chamada para ver quem estava na espera. Matheus. Seu chefe. Ela revirou os olhos e suspirou alto.

— Puta que o pariu, enfiou o horário comercial no cu. Só pode.

O telefone continuava vibrando. Poderia atender, mas e se a chamada com a companhia telefônica caísse? Depois de quase uma hora na linha, agora ela ia até o fim.

O trânsito andou, lentamente, mas os carros à sua frente se moveram o suficiente para que ela pudesse alegar que estava dirigindo na hora em que Matheus ligou. Nenhum chefe iria cobrar que ela infringisse a lei, não é mesmo?

Carla sentiu o olhar repreendedor da mãe em pensamento.

— Mentir é feio, Carla. Uma boa moça não mente.

Foda-se. Tecnicamente não estava mentindo. Estava, sim, dirigindo e a ligação no viva-voz estava na espera há tanto tempo que se tornara uma péssima escolha musical no rádio.

Ela deu o sinal para a direita e virou em uma rua menos

movimentada. O telefone parou de tocar e seus ombros relaxaram alguns milímetros. Mentalmente, repassou todos os prazos e tarefas que tinha para entregar no trabalho. Estava tudo em dia. O que quer que Matheus tivesse para falar não poderia ser urgente.

Ou poderia?

O supermercado apareceu no final da rua e Carla imaginou que vivia o filme de ação mais chato da história. O trânsito fluindo como estava, em menos de cinco minutos entraria no estacionamento do mercado. Seria atendida antes disso?

O celular vibrou com mais uma ligação de Matheus. Carla olhou para o relógio. Seis e trinta e quatro. Ainda poderia ser considerado horário comercial? Não deveria uma profissional de redes sociais estar disponível 24 horas por dia? Afinal, as redes não param nunca.

Carla entrou no estacionamento do mercado e procurou por uma vaga. A chamada de Matheus parou de tocar. Mais rápido do que da vez anterior. Contudo, o alívio durou pouco desta vez. Assim que estacionou o carro a música de Beethoven se encerrou bruscamente. Carla percebeu como tinha sido burra.

Garagem nunca tem sinal de celular, muito menos de uma companhia telefônica que não consegue nem levar sinal decente até o nono andar do prédio no centro da cidade onde ela mora.

Meu Deus! Sua casa está praticamente na mesma altura do poste na rua. Como pode ser assim tão difícil?

Ela teve vontade de chorar de raiva. Da companhia telefônica, do chefe, das redes sociais que ainda vão tornar os robôs líderes mundiais e fazer com que a única música que possamos ouvir seja *Für Elise*.

Mas pensou em Isabela, pensou na mãe e pensou no filho que carregava dentro de si, ainda tão pequenininho que só ela sabia que estava ali. Não havia contado para ninguém, nem para o ex-marido. Como contar para o homem de quem você está se divorciando não faz nem um mês que vocês terão mais um filho juntos?

Carla respirou fundo, engoliu as lágrimas, pegou o celular, os fones de ouvido, a bolsa e as chaves do carro. Subiu até o mercado e ligou para Matheus.

O carro novo, as compras e dois, dois, filhos não se pagam com sonhos.

3º movimento — Isabela

— Vó, o que significa Ode? — perguntou Isabela, lendo o título da partitura musical à sua frente, já que as notas lhe eram confusas demais.

— Significa homenagem.

— Então Beethoven escreveu uma homenagem à alegria? Em forma de música?

— Isso mesmo — respondeu a avó com um sorriso.

Isabela gostava de ver a avó sorrir, principalmente quando o sorriso vinha acompanhado desse olhar de admiração para ela.

— Beethoven não é aquele cara que ficou surdo?

— Ele mesmo. Agora chega de conversa fiada e toque a música.

A menina escondeu uma reação de irritação e voltou a martelar as notas no piano. Ela gostava dessa expressão, martelar. Uma vez o afinador havia visitado a avó em um dia de aula e ela havia visto o piano aberto. As teclas se ligavam a vários martelinhos e, quando a gente tocava, eles martelavam as cordas e saía o som.

Era muito parecido com o que ela sentia que acontecia em seu cérebro. Cada nota que aprendia era martelada lá dentro como se fosse prego. E Isabela se esforçava muito, pois sua leitura musical era péssima e ela não queria que a avó percebesse.

Queria o olhar de admiração, não mais uma aula interminável sobre aquelas linhas, rabiscos e bolinhas que não faziam sentido nenhum.

— Pronto. — disse Isabela assim que a última nota ecoou pela sala.

A avó sorriu amavelmente.

— Não, não, Isa. Nunca está pronto. Um bom músico precisa tocar várias e várias vezes e, mesmo assim, a música nunca estará perfeita.

Isabela recebeu a novidade com espanto. Uma vida toda trabalhando a mesma música? Por isso que ninguém ouve mais música clássica hoje em dia!

Cadê a variedade? A diversão?

— A Júlia, minha melhor amiga, começou a fazer aula de violão, sabia, vó?

A avó assentiu e virou as páginas da partitura para o início novamente.

— Ela disse que vai levar para a escola um dia para tocar pra gente as músicas que ela está aprendendo. Ela disse que já tocou a música da Mirabel, sabe?

— De quem?

— Da Mirabel. Do filme da Disney.

— A vaca?

— Não! Essa é a Clarabela, vó, não tem nada a ver. A Mirabel é a princesa nova. Da família Madrigal. É uma família que tem poderes. Ela tem uma irmã chamada Isabela, que nem eu, e uma avó que manda em todo mundo . . .

— Aham. Do início. Vamos. Tem que trabalhar esses primeiros compassos.

Isabela revirou os olhos.

— A gente não pode tocar outra música depois? Pode ser do Beethoven também, não precisa ser da Disney.

Qualquer coisa seria mais legal do que a mesma música que tocava desde os seis anos de idade. Ela já era quase uma mocinha, não era? Podia aprender coisas novas. Ela podia procurar a música na internet.

Era só pegar o celular.

A avó fechou os olhos e massageou as têmporas. Isabela viu como ela estava cansada e ficou triste por chateá-la.

— Tudo bem. Vou tocar de novo. O que você acha que precisa melhorar?

— Do compasso três ao cinco. — respondeu a avó, abrindo os olhos e indicando a partitura — Você está tocando com muita força. A música começa alegre, mas você precisa transmitir isso com delicadeza, não com força.

A menina repetiu os compassos indicados, procurando sentir a música e a força de seus dedos nas teclas. Com sua atenção focada na delicadeza que a avó pedira, ela tocou várias notas erradas e dissonantes no meio da melodia. Isabela sentiu seu estômago revirar e perdeu a paciência.

— Merda! — exclamou, macetando as teclas do piano com o punho.

— Isabela! — gritou a avó, fazendo com que a menina desse um pulo no banco do piano.

— Desculpa, vó. — respondeu, abaixando a cabeça e acariciando as teclas com os dedos. Sua avó gostava muito daquele piano. Ela não deveria ter descontado sua raiva nele.

— Isabela, essa palavra é muito feia. Você não pode falar assim.

A garota olhou para a senhora, confusa. Ouvia a palavra dentro de casa várias vezes. Ela mesma já a dissera quando estivera particularmente irritada, como quando topou com o dedinho no pé da cama. A mãe nunca a havia repreendido.

— Desculpa . . . — Mesmo assim, se havia ofendido a avó ela deveria pedir desculpas. Isabela sabia respeitar a todos, principalmente os mais velhos.

— Não repita mais isso.

— Desculpa, vó.

A senhora assentiu com uma expressão firme.

— Mais uma vez.

Isabela obedeceu, pensando que, se Beethoven ainda estivesse vivo, ela iria queimar todas as suas partituras para que nenhuma outra avó obrigasse netinhas a tocarem tantas vezes as mesmas músicas chatas.

Quando terminou, percebeu que a sala estava mais escura. O dia estava virando noite lá fora e isso era bom. A avó nunca continuava as aulas depois que o sol ia embora.

— Muito bem! Agora sim. Viu como que com paciência a gente

acerta? — disse a senhora, passando a mão carinhosamente pelos cabelos da neta.

Isabela assentiu.

— Agora feche o piano e venha me ajudar a fechar as janelas. Cuidado para não prender o dedo! Daqui a pouco sua mãe está de volta para te buscar e você ainda tem que fazer sua tarefa de casa.

A menina obedeceu.

— Vó, você gosta de Beethoven?

Isabela esperava um "sim" imediato, mas a avó hesitou.

— Ele foi um gênio da música — respondeu enfim.

— Mas você gosta dele? — Isabela cobriu as teclas do piano com uma tira de tecido vermelho.

— São músicas lindas. — disse a avó, fechando as cortinas.

— E se você me ensinasse mais uma? Do Beethoven. — Isabela fechou o piano, cuidando para não prender os dedos no processo.

A avó sorriu. Era difícil enxergar a expressão exata no rosto dela por conta da penumbra que envolvia a sala. Se estivesse claro o suficiente, talvez Isabela poderia ter identificado um olhar de tristeza no rosto da avó. Ou talvez não, pois ela ainda era nova.

— Eu só sei essa, minha filha — confessou a senhora baixinho.

E, para Isabela, tudo fez sentido.

— Tudo bem, vó. A gente pode aprender uma música nova juntas.

As duas saíram da sala e Isabela fechou a porta, como sempre.

Fugue n° 9

by Luiza Guimarães

1st movement — Leila

Leila played on the piano the empty notes of Beethoven's Ninth Symphony. Ever since she started her studies, when she was three years old, the notes for "Ode to Joy" had been hammered in her brain. She never asked why. It was how things were meant to be. Good girls learned how to play the piano to entertain their future guests, in their future homes, which they would command with grace and without letting their efforts show.

Looking at her hardwood floors, the late afternoon sunlight filtering through her windows and the summer breeze gently blowing the white curtains inside, Leila could not feel anything other than failure. Where was the home filled with children and grandchildren that had been promised to her? With her loving stern husband, the help, and maybe one or two nosy neighbors?

In this living room there were just her and her portraits—photographs that seemed to mock the joyful song Leila insisted on hammering her fingers down on the piano keys for, in perfect mimicry of how she had learned each note so many years ago.

Portraits are a species in danger of being extinct. She visits her children and grandchildren every now and then and has already realized the age versus portrait ratio followed a descending geometric progression.

She blamed cell phones.

The music and her thoughts were invaded by the sound of a car horn by her front gate. Mentally, Leila cursed the driver with words that should never be spoken out loud by a respectable old lady, let alone directed towards her own daughter. But didn't she ask Carla to ring the bell? Was it so hard to hop out of her car? Greet her mother, have some coffee, maybe even talk a little?

Leila sighed, got up, and walked to the door, without minding to close her piano or the windows. She felt like a rebel and pictured her mother, scolding her from high up in her heavenly throne, next to Our Lord.

She opened the door and fought a small war against the arthritis on her fingers; they made the task of clicking the tiny buttons on the remote control to open her gate way harder than acceptable. Her granddaughter, Isabela, jumped out of the car with her school backpack.

The girl was wearing her shabby school uniform, with the same backpack as last year's. Leila had already probed her daughter to know if they were needing money, but her answers had been too vague for her to reach a conclusion. She would have liked to ask Carla directly, but it was not the polite thing to do.

The new car, with a shiny license plate, told her that maybe the girl was just sentimentally attached to the backpack.

— Grandma! — greeted Isabela, with a hug.

She was a loving child. Leila liked her hugs.

— Hi, my child! Isn't your mother coming in?

— No. She's in a hurry.

Leila waved to her daughter that, this time, at least went through the trouble to open the window to wave back. The car reversed and exited to the street as soon as the gate closed.

— I'm hungry grandma! — complained the girl.

— I'll make you some snacks. Then we will go to the piano.

— Ok!

So pretty and obedient. The little granddaughter of any grandmother's dreams. Isabela was nine years old and, ever since she was six, spent two afternoons a week studying the piano with her grandmother. Leila liked to spend her time with the little one and Carla took her time without the child to do whatever it is that mothers do by themselves nowadays.

True, the girl was distracted and agitated, but times have changed, thank God, because if Isabela were to one day rely on her musical skills to win herself a husband, Leila feared she would end up a spinster.

Even so, a bit of grace and delicate ways wouldn't hurt a girl. So it was twenty minutes for snacks and, afterwards, the old chords of "Ode to Joy" for the next few hours.

2nd movement — Carla

Why Beethoven? Why is it always Beethoven?

As she was driving, Carla was on hold to get help from her internet provider's customer service. She had signed a new contract so she could double her connection speed and work from home in the mornings, spending more time with her daughter, but ever since the signature it seemed the signal was traveling from the modem to her computer in the back of a tortoise.

She had already received two warnings from work, because she was authorized to work in-person for half of the day as long as she was available for the company when she was at home. Except it was simply impossible to join a video call with her current connection, and if spending more time with her daughter meant having to endure ... 40 minutes? Already? Anyway, if it meant having to endure 40 minutes listening to a robot performing Für Elise, so be it! Hopefully somebody would answer before she arrived at the supermarket.

Carla made a turn into one of the avenues congested with the afternoon traffic. The backlights of the cars were shining red against her eyes and the smell of smoke crept inside the car through the closed windows. A perfect reflex from her life, she thought: trapped among strangers who were also trying to get to their appointments, slowly suffocating with one other's smoke.

When she realized that neither the call nor the traffic were going to change in the next few minutes, Carla carefully opened Instagram. The call was still going. She hesitantly started to scroll her feed while the robot kept its musical performance on. She relaxed and stared at the screen in her hands.

There was her sister, vacationing at Disney World with the nephews. In the next post, her brother and his husband were somewhere exotic. Her college friend was celebrating a work promotion. Julia's mother,

Julia was her daughter's best friend, shared pictures of a child's birthday party on her stories.

Isa had not been invited to that party. Were there any problems in school? Or maybe the birthday girl was just a friend Julia knew from somewhere else? Carla had to remind herself, for the tenth or eleventh time that day, that Instagram was not real. The exotic place her brother and his husband had been was one of the many trails around the city that they go to every weekend. She had come with them once and almost died of boredom. They would stop every five minutes to take a photo and spent the rest of the walk complaining about mosquitoes, humidity, or the sharp climbs filled with pointy rocks.

Carla worked with content marketing for social media. Scrolling through her personal Instagram feed was an act of study at the same time as of procrastination. Yet another paradox that makes complete sense in the digital era.

She blamed cell phones.

The phone buzzed in her hands with a call on the wait line. Her immediate reaction was to look at her car's speaker, making sure the robot kept its symphony that was now 55 minutes and 49 seconds long. 50. 51. 52.

Relief. The call was not disconnected. She checked the caller ID. Matheus. Her boss. She rolled her eyes and sighed loudly.

— Motherfucker can shove business hours up his ass — she cursed at the phone screen, her fingers as far from the green button as possible. — That is the only reason why this asshole would call now.

The phone kept buzzing. She could pick it up, but what if she got disconnected with the internet provider? After one hour on the line, now she was going to make it through the end.

The traffic moved, slowly, but enough that she could claim to her boss that she was driving at the time he called. No boss would ever ask her to break the law, right?

Carla felt her mother's stern look in her mind.

"Lying is bad, Carla. Good girls don't lie."

Fuck it. Technically she was not lying. She was, yes, driving and the call on the speaker was on hold for so long that it had become a poor musical choice.

She signaled right and turned into a less crowded street. The phone stopped buzzing and her shoulders relaxed a few inches. Mentally, she ran through all the deadlines and tasks she needed to do for work. Everything was up-to-date. Whatever Matheus had to talk about could not be urgent.

Or could it be?

The supermarket was just at the end of the road and Carla imagined she was living the most boring action movie in the history of cinema. The transit, flowing as it was, would make it so she would reach the parking lot in less than five minutes. Would customer service get to her call before that?

The phone buzzed again with yet another call from Matheus. Carla looked at the clock. Five thirty-four. Could that still be considered business hours? Shouldn't a social media manager be available 24/7? After all, social media never sleeps.

Carla entered the parking lot and looked for a spot. Matheus' call stopped ringing quicker than before. However, the relief didn't last this time. As soon as she parked the car, the Beethoven song was cut off. Carla realized how stupid she was. There is never a phone signal in parking garages, let alone from a company that cannot deliver decent internet to the ninth floor in the building she lives in right in the center of the city! Oh my god! Her home was basically as tall as the street pole where all the internet cables were. How can that be so hard?

She felt like crying with anger. She was angry at the internet company, at her boss, at social media and the robots that will one day rule the world and make sure that the only music ever available to humanity is Für Elise.

But then she thought about Isabela, she thought about her mother, and she thought about the child she carried inside her body, so tiny that she was the only one who knew they were even there. She hadn't told anyone, not even her ex-husband. How do you tell the man you just started filing the divorce papers with that you will have another child together?

Carla took a deep breath, swallowed her tears, got her phone, her earbuds, her purse, and the car keys. She went up the stairs to the supermarket and called Matheus. A new car, her groceries, and two (two!) children don't get paid with dreams.

3rd movement — Isabela

— Grandma, what does Ode mean? — asked Isabela, reading the music's title on the sheet since the notes were too confusing.

— It means "in honor to."

— So Beethoven wrote a tribute to joy? In the form of a song?

— That's right — replied the grandmother, smiling.

Isabela liked to see her grandmother smile, especially when the smile came along with this admiring look directed towards her.

— Isn't Beethoven that guy that went deaf?

— That's him. Now enough talking and more playing.

The girl hid her annoyance and started hammering the notes on the piano again. She liked this expression, to hammer. Once a man came to tune her grandmother's piano during her class and she saw the open instrument. The keys were connected to many tiny little hammers and, when we played, they hammered the strings and the sound was made.

It was very similar to what she felt was happening to her brain. The sound of every note she learned was like a nail hammered to her mind. And Isabela worked very hard because her musical reading sucked and she didn't want her grandmother to notice. She wanted that admiring look, not yet another endless class about those lines and scribbles and circles that made no sense.

— Done — said Isabela as soon as the last note echoed through the room.

The grandmother smiled lovingly.

— No, no, Isa. It is never done. A good musician needs to play many, many times and, even so, the music will never be perfect.

Isabela received the news with shock. A whole life playing the same song? That is why nobody listens to classical music these days! Where is the fun in doing things all the same?

— My best friend Julia started taking guitar lessons. Did you know that, Grandma?

The grandmother nodded and turned the sheet music back to the beginning.

— She said she will take the guitar to school one day and play for us the songs she is learning. She said she knows how to play Mirabel's song, you know?

— Whose song?

— Mirabel's! From the Disney movie.

— The cow?

— No! That is Clarabelle, Grandma, duh! Mirabel is the new princess. She is a Madrigal. It is a family with superpowers. She has a sister named Isabela, like me, and a grandmother that bosses everyone around . . .

— Yes. Again. Let's go. We need to work on those first bars.

Isabela rolled her eyes.

— Can we play a different song later? It can be Beethoven's, it doesn't have to be Disney.

Anything would be more fun than playing the same song she's been playing ever since she was six. She was a big girl now, wasn't she? She could learn new things. She could google new songs.

All she had to do was check on her phone.

Her grandmother closed her eyes and massaged her temples. Isabela saw how tired the old woman was and she was sad to make her upset.

— That's alright. I'll play it again. What do you think needs to get better?

— From bar three to five — answered the grandmother, opening her eyes and pointing towards the music. — You are playing with too much strength. The music starts joyfully, but you need to transmit that delicately, not strongly.

The girl repeated the indicated bars, trying to feel the music and how heavy her fingers were on the keys. All her focus was on the delicate aspect her grandmother had requested, so she kept playing many wrong notes. The dissonance made Isabela's stomach turn and she lost her patience.

— Shit! — the girl exclaimed, closing her fists against the piano keys.

— Isabela! — screamed her grandmother, making the girl jump on her stool.

— I am sorry, Grandma — she replied, bowing her head and caressing the keys with her fingers. Her grandmother liked that piano very much. She should not have laid her anger on it.

— Isabela, that is a very bad word. You can't talk like that.

The girl looked at the old lady, confused. She used to hear that word a lot at home. She had said it herself when she was annoyed or hurt, like that time when she bumped her little toe against the dinner table. Her mother never told her it was bad.

— Sorry . . . — even so, if she had offended her grandmother she should apologize. Isabela knew how to be respectful of everyone, especially of her elders.

— Never say that again.

— I am sorry, Grandma.

The old woman nodded with a firm expression on her face.

— Once more.

Isabela obeyed, thinking that, if Beethoven had still been alive, she would burn every single one of his music writings so no other grandmother could make their poor little granddaughters play the same boring song so many times.

When she was done, she noticed the room was darker. The day was turning into night outside and that was good. Her grandmother never continued with her classes after the sun left.

— Well done! Now that is good. See how patience helps us get things right? — Said the lady, running her fingers tenderly through her granddaughter's hair.

Isabela nodded.

— Now close the piano and come help me close the windows as well. Be careful not to hurt your fingers! Soon your mother will be back here to pick you up and you still have homework to do.

The girl complied.

— Grandma, do you like Beethoven?

Isabela was expecting an immediate "yes", but her grandmother hesitated.

— He was a musical genius — she replied at last.

— But do you like him? — Isabela covered the piano keys with a red velvet strip.

— He wrote beautiful songs — said the grandmother, closing the curtains.

— What if you taught me another one? By Beethoven? — Isabela closed the lid on the piano's keys, minding not to hurt her fingers.

Her grandmother smiled. It was hard to see the exact expression on her face because of the dimming sunlight. If it had been bright enough, maybe Isabela could have identified sadness in her grandmother's eyes. Or maybe she wouldn't have. She was still young afterall.

— All I know is this one, my child — confessed the lady in a low voice.

And, to Isabela, everything made sense.

— That's ok, Grandma. We can learn a new one together.

They both left the room and Isabela closed the door, like always.

Contributor Bios

Kimberly Anderson is a Publishing Master's student at Pace University and holds Bachelor's degrees in English and Gender & Women's Studies from California State University, Northridge. Whether she is writing poetry or editing other's work, she is passionate about connecting people through shared experiences. In her free time, she likes to read a wide variety of genres, play soccer, and support women's sports. Kimberly resides in Los Angeles County, California with her family and two dogs and no, she won't stop talking about why the West Coast is the best coast.

Nicolina Barone is pursuing a five-year combined degree program at Pace University for a BA in Writing and Rhetoric and an MS in Publishing. She is completing the program a year early and will be graduating in May 2024. She is the president and managing editor of *CHROMA*, Pace University's Pleasantville campus literary and arts magazine. She is a freelance editor at WebMD Ignite and just completed an internship at Rizzoli International Publications. Nicolina has always had a deep love and passion for words and self-published a poetry book in 2020 called Serendipity. She is currently working on the second draft of her 65,000-word romantic fiction novel. She is the recipient of the Summer 2023 Provost's Student-Faculty Undergraduate Creative Inquiry Award. She is so excited to share her work with the world.

Camille Daniels is a first-year graduate student at Dyson College of the MS in Publishing program. She was introduced to poetry in the sixth grade and never looked back. It became the thing that caused her to fall into deep liking and eventually love writing by first loving words, spelling, and language. It has helped her to develop and find her voice while also being a form of therapy. She is honored to be part of this historic first issue of this new publication. It reminds her why she's now studying publishing and likes to write. It is the freedom to express herself and share what is on her mind that brings her joy. It empowers her to continue to write poetry for herself and share it when it counts.

Shea Dunlop is in her first year of the MS in Publishing program, taking classes online while working full-time at Killington Ski Resort in her home state of Vermont. She lives in a ramshackle ski house with eight roommates, her boyfriend, and her cat, Charles. This spring, she'll be bringing the "small town girl moves to big city" trope to life, relocating to Brooklyn and diving into the publishing world head-first. An avid audiobook listener, she would love to work close to them, but is also interested in learning more about special sales and subrights. In her free time, you can find her in the gym, playing board games, and reading fantasy/speculative fiction.

James Brandon Fizer is a second-year MS Publishing student and graduate of the University of Michigan. With exactly 20 years between finishing undergrad and starting graduate school at Pace University, taking in campus culture has been both cozily familiar and startlingly new. As a working writer for the majority of his adult life, Mr. Fizer has worked in broadcast and magazine journalism, advertising copy and, most recently, financial services digital content creation. He decided to pursue the graduate program in Publishing because he felt like his career was moving farther and farther away from why he became a writer in the first place. That's because his biggest dream has always been to publish a novel someday. His submission here pushes him closer to that true calling.

Amber Grell is a part-time MS in Publishing student with dreams of working as a literary agent upon graduation; she currently works as a copy editor and proofreader in a corporate real estate office. Originally from Wyoming, Minnesota, she earned a Bachelor's degree in both English (Creative Writing) and Communications (Journalism) from Adelphi University, graduating Magna Cum Laude with honors. She recently started a lending library at her apartment building where she acts as the Resident Librarian, is a member of the New York Public Library, is a member of the New York Book Forum, considers herself a YA junkie, and aims to read 120 books annually. Amber finds happiness at home with her cat, Riley Matthews Grell, surrounded by dessert and new books.

Luiza Guimarães is a Brazilian journalist and storyteller. She was an avid fantasy reader and writer growing up. Nowadays, her favorite genres are romance and contemporary fiction, especially the ones produced by Latin American authors. She is part of the Escreviventes collective in Brazil, a group of women writers who help each other develop their work. Luiza is currently an intern at Lantern Publishing & Media, and the Editor-in-Chief of *The Publishing Lab*. She is very excited to graduate from the Pace Publishing MS program in the spring of 2024, and is looking forward to working with stories that can contribute to shaping a safer, equitable, and more sustainable world.

Shianne Henion (writing as Shay Blackthorn) is trying her best. As a fantasy girlie living in the Hudson Valley, she spends most of her time in fictional places. Other times, she is romanticizing the world around her, the life she leads, and the many thoughts that swirl inside her brain. Shay likes cheese, coffee, and cats, in that order (otherwise known as the three Cs). With a BS in English, journalism, and creative writing (she is obtaining her Master's degree for publishing), she only knows sentences, and how to have a mental breakdown while remaining productive.
You can find Shay on her Instagram (shayblackthorn), her bookstagram (thornsandbooks), and probably in a coffee shop about to order her fourth cup.

Nina Hook is a current student at Pace University NYC, completing her BA in English and MS in Publishing through the 4/1 program. From Yuma, Arizona, she moved to NYC to pursue her zeal for writing and publishing! With an emphasis in creative writing, she loves to write poetry and creative nonfiction. She wants to further her career in publishing through editorial, media and marketing, and subrights efforts. In her spare time, Nina reads (of course), plays tennis, and spends time wandering around the city.

Shannon Huurman is originally from Dallas, Texas, currently living in New York City. Huurman graduated from Fordham University Rose Hill in 2022 and is now pursuing a Masters in Publishing at Pace University.

Kaitlyn Keel graduated with a Bachelor's Degree in Public Relations from Carthage College in Kenosha, WI in 2021. In her spare time, you can find her reading queer fiction or watering her beloved plants. *Everything I Know Leads Me Back to You* is her first published piece.

Valentina López-Pérez is a first-year student in the MS in Publishing program at Pace University, hailing from Colombia and currently residing in New York City. Her passion for books has been a guiding force since her early years, leading her to pursue a major in Literature at Los Andes University in Bogotá, Colombia. This academic journey solidified her desire and determination to become part of the world of publishing. Beyond books and reading, she enjoys photography, language learning, and handicrafts. As an international student, she has a particular interest in books in translation, aspiring to increase and introduce voices from multiple corners of the globe. Valentina envisions her role in the industry as a means to build bridges between cultures, sparking conversations about traditions, cultural exchange, and the experiences and perspectives that shape our worldview.

Michaela MacFarran is a New York City based writer, specializing in lesbian-centric playwriting and prose. She is a second year graduate student in the Pace University Publishing program. When not writing, she can be found hanging out on her couch with her girlfriend, Emily, and their cat, Viola, watching *The X Files*.
Email: michaelamacfarran@gmail.com | Instagram: @micinadadcap

Jack Niemczyk is a writer and comedian living in the East Village of New York. He refers to himself as a champagne socialite and often uses his experiences in the nightlife scene of New York in his writing. As a proud homosexual, Jack embraces the intersectionality and queerness of life and love in a city as eccentric as New York. He is currently a student at Pace University finishing his undergrad in Creative Writing and working towards a Master's in Publishing.

Hannah Penn is a current student in Pace's Publishing Program. She graduated with her Bachelor's in English and Creative Writing from the University at Albany in 2021. Her ultimate goal is to work as an editorial assistant with a focus on contemporary fiction. This is her first time being published and she is beyond thrilled to be a part of the project. Hannah is a Rochester, NY native and spends much of her time exploring the surrounding area. One of her favorite expeditions was stumbling into an open mic at a local café where she ended up sharing a few of her pieces. Alongside open mics, Hannah is a fan of attending local music events, hiking, and spending time with her cat named Goose.

Isha Repal is an international student from India currently pursuing her Master's in the Publishing program at Pace University. With a Bachelor's in Computer Science, her love for books and stories pushed her towards NYC in hopes of publishing many unearthed diamonds. She can be found in cozy nooks of coffee shops and bookstores as she trains her pen to join the editorial or the production department.

Elyse Rosenberg is in her final year in the MS Publishing program at Pace with dreams of working in publicity when she graduates. She received her Bachelor's at Central Connecticut State University where she created her own major, Movement & Mind, combining dance and psychology. She became a Zumba® instructor in 2011, which she still teaches to this day, and is a retired professional ballroom dancer. Elyse has enjoyed photography as a hobby since she learned how to develop her own photos in a darkroom at camp. When she's not outside photographing landscapes, Elyse can be found baking and curled up with her cat, Lizzie McGuire Rosenberg, while enjoying mystery and historical fiction books.

Katie Schwab is an aspiring writer and recent graduate of the MS in Publishing program at Pace University in New York City. Born and raised in Northern California, she spent her childhood and teen years fostering her creativity and entertaining friends and family through reading, writing, and theater. After publishing her graduate thesis, "Publishing Queer Literature: A Comparison Between the Adult and Young Adult Markets from the Cold War to Present Day" in *Publishing Research Quarterly*, Schwab has made it her goal to create and uplift other queer stories and storytellers. She currently lives in Santa Ana, CA, hard at work on her debut novel.

Kayleigh Woltal is a first-year MS in Publishing student pursuing a career as a designer in publishing. Before coming to Pace, Kayleigh attended Fordham University at Lincoln Center, receiving a BA in New Media and Digital Design with a minor in English. After graduating from Fordham, Kayleigh began volunteering as a graphic designer at *grain of salt* magazine where she works on editorial and social media graphics as well as layout for print zines. Kayleigh has always loved to read, write, and create and is excited to be part of *The Publishing Lab*.

The Publishing Lab Team

Professor Manuela Soares | Faculty Advisor

Professor Eileen Kreit | Faculty Advisor

Luiza Guimarães | Editor-in-Chief

Shianne Henion | Editorial & Production

Kaitlyn Keel | Editorial & Production

Amber Grell | Editorial

Harshdeep Kaur | Editorial

Sam Semerau | Editorial

Kristen Mejia | Editorial

Pand Milo | Marketing Coordinator

Mary Duffy | Marketing

Elyse Rosenberg | Marketing

Kayleigh Woltal | Cover Photo & Designer

PACE
UNIVERSITY

MS IN PUBLISHING PROGRAM

Get Ahead in Publishing

We prepare tomorrow's publishing leaders with internships, scholarships, and mentoring.

Cutting-Edge

Current industry trends move at a fast clip. Our forward-thinking graduate degree allows students to learn hands-on and explore topics such as:

- Acquisition and sub-rights
- Content creation and editing
- Marketing and publicity
- Sales and distribution
- Finance and legal
- Production and design
- E-books and digital media
- Comics and graphic novels
- Artficial Intelligence
- Social Media

Comprehensive

From manuscript to finished product, in both print and digital media, you'll be equipped with in-depth knowledge needed to build a successful career.

- Pace offers scholarship opportunities to finance your education
- We offer in-person and online classes that set students on track to graduate in two years
- We send two students to the London Book Fair, Bologna Book Fair, and/or the Frankfurt Book Fair each year

Connected

Our top-notch faculty are industry professionals who bring their expertise to the classroom.

- Students cultivate professional connections with industry leaders through one-to-one mentorships, internships, guest lectures, and industry-sponsored events
- Our alumni have gone on to work at literary agencies, digital media, advertising companies, and publishing houses large and small

Creating Community

We offer unique opportunities for students to come together and collaborate, including:

- *The Publishing Lab,* an annual student-run anthology of student creative work
- Dedicated publishing student space with a computer lab and lounge area
- In-person and online student events
- Our one-to-one mentorship program pairs student-protégés with industry professionals for one semester
- Build your network of publishing professionals

Contact the Office of Graduate Admissions:
graduateadmissions@pace.edu or call (212) 346-1531

Apply today or attend an information session:
www.pace.edu/grad

WORDS WE USE

A Glossary and Reference Guide for Publishing and Media

This glossary of publishing terms is for anyone who is interested in a career in publishing and digital media or those already working in the field. The words used in publishing and media are a distinct and essential part of our ability to communicate with each other. Language is not static and the language in publishing has grown, changed, and continues to evolve in our digital world. Compiled by industry experts, this book provides a wide-ranging and inclusive compilation of terms that will assist anyone interested in learning more about publishing and media.

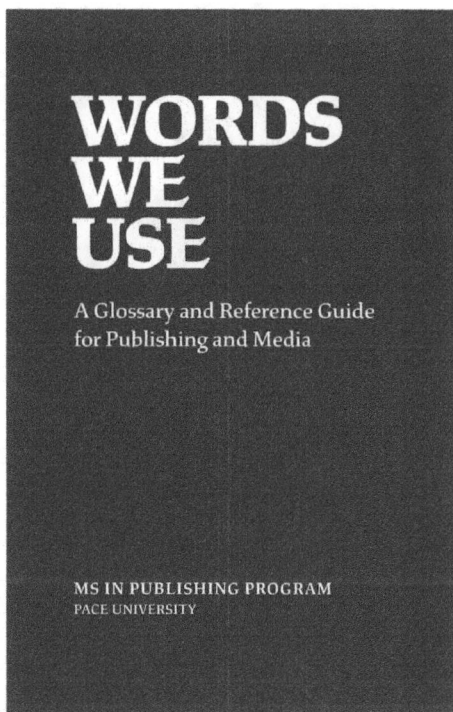

WORDS WE USE

A Glossary and Reference Guide for Publishing and Media

MS IN PUBLISHING PROGRAM
PACE UNIVERSITY

For more information or to order *Words We Use* and other titles published by Pace University Press, please visit www.pace.edu/press.

PACE
UNIVERSITY
PRESS

Pace University Press
41 Park Row
New York, New York 10038
212 346 1405

The first volume of *The Publishing Lab*
was published in Spring 2024 by Pace University Press

Cover and interior layout by Kayleigh Woltal
The anthology was typeset in PT Serif and Century Gothic
and printed by Lightning Source

Pace University Press
Director: Manuela Soares
Faculty Advisor: Eileen Kreit
Design Consultant: Joseph Caserto
Production Assistant: Lucely Garcia

Graduate Assistants: Erin Hurley and Kayleigh Woltal
Graduate Student Aide: Elizabeth Abrams

www.ingramcontent.com/pod-product-compliance
Lightning Source LLC
Chambersburg PA
CBHW061733270326
41928CB00011B/2212